The DRE Reader

The DRE Reader
A Sourcebook in Education and Ministry

**Edited by
Maria Harris**

A PACE Book

Saint Mary's Press
Christian Brothers Publications
Winona, Minnesota

Cover design by Roderick Robertson, FSC

ISBN: 0-88489-124-0
Library of Congress Catalog Card Number: 80-52059

Copyright 1980 by Saint Mary's Press,
Terrace Heights, Winona, Minnesota 55987

Contents

(Some of) The Many Roles of the DRE: Theologian,
Executive, Administrator, Spiritual Director

PART TWO

Reports from the Field

Counsel from the Field

Introduction

Since 1970, Saint Mary's Press has published over 500 articles in PACE (PACE, acronym for Professional Approaches for Christian Educators, is the name of the monthly publication appearing since 1970). All of them, in one way or another, are applicable to Directors of Religious Education. My task, in editing this collection, was to read these articles and select those most pertinent to the DRE. The task proved difficult, not because the articles were too few, but because they were too many. In presenting those finally selected, I express regret this book cannot be three times its present length.

Such limitation, however, forced me to develop and to adhere to three criteria. First, I chose articles directly related to the identity and profession of DRE. This meant I had to leave out many excellent pieces which were more general, such as commentaries on the NCD, suggestions on education for justice, and essays concerned with innumerable specialized areas such as family ministry, youth, attention to the separated and divorced, programs in adult education, and prayer.

Secondly, I chose not to include "how to" articles or descriptions of successful approaches because of the plethora of such articles in our books and journals; for these, readers can peruse the pages of PACE themselves and choose the ones most applicable to their own situations. In contrast, we still have very little substantive, sustained, and consistent reflection on the identity and profession of the DRE of the kind demonstrated in this volume. To the best of my knowledge the only two books other than this one dealing directly with the DRE profession in Catholic circles are Joseph Neiman's **Coordinators** (Saint Mary's Press, 1971) and my own **The DRE Book** (Paulist, 1976).

Finally, I wanted to select articles which from the very beginning mirrored the self-understanding of DREs as that understanding has grown to the present day. I hoped the mirroring would provide something of a history of the profession. In this I was not disappointed, and in the ordering of the book, I hope this history and this self-understanding is apparent.

In reading the evidence supplied by PACE authors over the past decade, my own judgment is that "DRE" refers to someone who works in two professions: religious education and ministry. However, the relation of the two remains unclear. For some DREs, the two are in tension, for others they are easily separable. For the largest number, education appears to be a subset of ministry, or an element within it, although for a sizable minority, DRE (despite the terminology) does not refer to someone in education at all, but to a person engaged in pastoral ministry. Additional complexity characterizes the profession since, within both education and ministry, the DRE is usually asked to take on roles such as theologian, teacher, administrator, spiritual director, and so on. These issues provide the framework ordering the first section of the book: identity, religious education, ministry, the two professions and the many roles of the DRE.

The other historical occurrence is the growth of self-understanding among DREs, often in relationship to Diocesan Associations of DREs. This is represented in a number of the articles "From the Field" which appeared in PACE as a result of persons working as DREs or as Diocesan Coordinators of DRE groups. I can only applaud this occurrence, hope for its continued and healthy growth, and urge those who have not yet established communal bonds to seriously consider doing so, not only within, but across Diocesan boundaries. In addition, I urge those who have not published accounts of their work to begin—I regret we did not have more articles such as Richelle Koller's, Daryl Olszewski's, Janet Bennett's, or Mary Margaret Funk's from which to choose. Perhaps the next book for DREs could be a corporate text, co-authored by DRE Associations across the land.

My hope for this book is expressed in its subtitle. It is offered as a sourcebook to DREs throughout this country who are struggling to carve a profession, to create bonds of sisterhood and brotherhood, and to clarify their identity—DREs who love their work and their church. It is also intended as a thank you to them for bearing the burden and heat, the joy and the celebration of the last decade, and as a symbol which says: Rejoice, you are not alone. I hope people will read it quietly, carefully, and without hurry, and then use it as the base of communal study, learning, and action.

In conclusion I offer thanks to all those at Saint Mary's Press for their continuing support of DREs, especially Brother Damian Steger, Steve Nagel, and Sheila Moriarty O'Fahey, who have contributed so much editorial and publishing skill; to each of the authors for the originality and strength of their essays; and to the staff of the Boston Archdiocesan Religious Education Office for gracious hospitality to me during my work on this book. I owe the greatest debt of gratitude, however, to Mary Perkins Ryan, editor of PACE. To her I wish not only to say thank you, but to acknowledge publicly that in my judgment she, more than any woman in the U.S. Catholic Church, has inspired the twofold vocation of religious education and ministry described in this book.

Maria Harris
Brookline, Massachusetts
July, 1980

PART ONE

Who Are We: Five Views

1
The Coordinator—
A Functional Definition

Thomas Walters

Many pastors and parishioners, as well as coordinators themselves, today seek a better understanding of the coordinator's role in the Church. They are curious about the skills and attitudes, if any, that he or she brings to the work. They wonder about the assumptions coordinators make and the values they develop, and they are especially interested in sizing up these attitudes and values. Do they form a consistent pattern? Are they stimulating? What effects do they have?

Many of these questions cannot even be formulated in most instances because there is no basic understanding of the term "coordinator." Many diocesan and parish job descriptions would be good illustrations of this fact. It seems that what has been forgotten is that since Christianity became institutionalized—that is, since the Church came into existence—it assumed the responsibility of having continually to specify and clarify the various functions and functionaries within the organization. In this article then, I will attempt to define the term "coordinator" functionally by showing its relation, past and present, to the organization that is the Church.

The dramatic and almost instantaneous demise of the Catholic school in America took the organizational Church by surprise. Until a few years ago the total thrust of the Church's educational ministry was focused on buttressing the faltering status quo of the Catholic school system and little attention was paid to developing viable out-of-school structures for religious education. It was in the early and middle sixties, when Catholic schools first began to suffer a noticeable drop in enrollments and more and more schools were experiencing deeper and deeper debts, that parishes were forced to consider alternate modes of religious instruction. CCD had to this point been considered the limbo of religious education. It was the place for the children of the poor souls who couldn't afford to send their children to the Catholic schools or the heretical souls who chose not to enroll their children. It was far from heaven but not quite hell. Yet as the non-Catholic-school numbers continued to multiply and existing CCD programs could no longer cope, either organizationally or educationally, with the increasing number of students, the job of coordinator came into being. It was born of a need—the need for an educational programmer and administrator. But in most instances the parishes affected were unable to assess the true nature of this need and sought a solution by appealing to the well-intentioned but untrained volunteer.

In the late sixties and early seventies, when Catholic schools experienced their greatest drop in registrations and many schools were forced to close, out-of-school religious instruction became a central issue in most parishes. The need for qualified personnel began to be obvious, but the people to fill the positions weren't. So with more schools closing and the teacher market glutted, many teachers, secular and religious, chose to become coordinators. As a result, many entered the profession who had no concept of the tasks involved. The universities which were specializing in cate-chetics at the time were caught in a transitional stage and were not sure what they were preparing students for. And so they opted to train theology teachers and not educational programmers and ad-ministrators. The results were divisive on the parish level. Many a parish experiencing the need for a coordinator, someone to design and administer non-parochial school religious education, found itself confronted with a gifted teacher or a theology major who was lacking in the theory and administrative skills required for educa-tional programming. At the same time because he or she—as well as those who hired them—too frequently had no clear vision of the coordinator's role, many coordinators found themselves in con-tinual conflict with the priests and/or the parish. They were often overextended and working in areas where they lacked competency.

What is becoming clearer now is the reason why coordinators were needed in the first place. It was not to develop theology—the Church retained her theologians; it was not to destroy the Church. The existing organization merely sought administrative assistance; and the coordinator was hired to provide viable struc-tures for educating the parish unit. Anything else was secondary.

In the coordinator's position, the area of competence was and is educational programming and administration. Coordinators need to understand the various theories of learning and be able to trans-late that knowledge into effective programs. They will constantly be called upon to make decisions, to pass professional judgment and to offer advice, but they will be asked to do this as adminis-trators and specialists in the field of education—not as theologians and teachers.

This is not to imply that a solid background in theology, Scripture, and liturgy is unimportant or unnecessary but that it is, without an equally strong background in the behavioral sciences, inadequate. At the end of this article I have listed some non-theological questions that I feel should be, but seldom are, asked and answered by coordinators.

Coordination is a function. It is the act of bringing together materials and personnel so that they operate with the least amount of friction and with the maximum use of potential. To coordinate effectively is to order harmoniously. Within the parish context, coordination is the directing of materials and personnel to result in an effective and smoothly operating program in religious education.

Defining the role of **the coordinator as educational programmer and administrator** does not confine the role but clarifies it and actually expands its horizons. If a parish or individual uses the term in a precise and meaningful way, there is less likelihood of confusion and hard feelings at evaluation time. Also, if specialization is to take place, a definite starting point is required. That point would be educational design and administration. So the coordinator as a specialist would be understood as an "educational programmer and administrator" who specializes in a particular area, e.g., adult learners, adolescent value-clarification, sacramental preparation . . . the possiblities would be numberless.

If people in the Church today are to understand the coordinator's role, coordinators themselves must agree on the tasks involved. Once this understanding is achieved, the profession will attain a certain legitimacy. The skills and attitudes required for the job will be more easily identified and practiced. Consistency and effectiveness, the hallmarks of any profession, will be possible and in the long run the whole community will profit.

QUESTIONS FOR REFLECTION

(1) What is the nature and scope of the learning process? (2) What theory of learning do I espouse? (3) How do the principles of this theory affect my program? (4) Are my administrative decisions consistent with my theory of learning? (5) Where is my program inconsistent with this theory? (6) How do I justify these inconsistencies? (7) What type of person will my program produce? (8) Upon what data do I make this statement? (9) What prerequisites do I set for teacher recruitment and selection? (10) Do these prerequisites reflect my theory of learning? (11) Does the text or lack of text re-

flect my theory of learning? (12) Is the criteria I use for evaluation theoretically sound?

This article first appeared in PACE in 1973. The author, THOMAS WALTERS, was religious education coordinator at St. Timothy's Parish in Trenton, Michigan, having received his M.A. from the University of Detroit. He is presently Supervisor of Evaluations for the Religious Education Office in the Archdiocese of Detroit.

2

The DRE for Parishes Serious about Total Religious Education

Mary Margaret Funk

American Catholics are known for being serious about religious education. After three generations of elementary, secondary, and college experience, the aim now is to reach into adult stages of development. Parishes serious about Total Religious Education (TRE) hire Directors of Religious Education. In Indianapolis, like other dioceses, the Archdiocesan Board of Education recently passed a policy recommending each parish hire a DRE. The following presents three reasons behind the decision, but presumes parishes are committed to TRE—understood as meaning continual religious education of all age levels in the three dimensions of message, community, and service (TJD 1973).

DEFINITION AND ROLE

The DRE is hired by the board to organize, facilitate, and evaluate both formal and informal programs. This would require that the DRE be skilled in administration, theology, and education. As an administrator, the DRE would need to set goals, plan, evaluate, budget, report, hire and maintain staff, conduct meetings, minimize conflicts, and inspire creativity. The DRE needs to integrate in the curriculum the theology promoted by Vatican II and recent documents which call for doctrinal comprehensiveness and relevant communication. More than being a teacher him/herself, he/she should enable other teachers to effectively use a developmental curriculum, A-V resources, and the best of contemporary educational theory. The particular needs of the parish will determine to some extent the kinds of ability and experience the DRE should have.

POSITION OF THE DRE IN THE PARISH STRUCTURE

The DRE relates to the Parish Council in two ways. First, the DRE "officially" relates to the Parish Council through the Education Commission which is the same as the Board of Catholic Education.

Second, the DRE could be used for in-service and renewal kinds of educational experiences for the Parish Council. The DRE with his/her background in education, theology, and liturgy is often the best "resource" person for these necessary sessions. Also, since religious education is not just something to learn but something one **does**, the DRE needs to work closely with the other Commissions to achieve communication and integration with social and liturgical activities.

The DRE can assist the Board to perform its major functions in the following ways:

1) The DRE can be a resource person to help the Board develop its objectives.
2) The DRE is the administrator for Total Religious Education just as the principal is the administrator for the academic education in the school. Together they form the administrative team for Total Catholic Education (religious and academic education). Only if a Board has someone to implement its policies does it function as a board rather than a discussion club. The DRE can also initiate policies regarding religious education as the principal initiates policies for the school.
3) After the board passes the policy, the DRE decides on the best way the policy can be carried out. He/she keeps the board informed through process reports. As an administrator the DRE plans, organizes, implements, and develops the religion programs with consultation of those involved.
4) A final evaluation can be made by the Board of Education based on the written report supplied by the DRE at the end

of the year. The board can then see to what extent the programs met their original objective.

The principal, where there is a school, and the DRE work as a team with the pastors of the parish. Since the DRE and the principal are both hired by the board they should be peers by position, salary, education, and experience.

For Total Catholic Education to happen, it is essential that the DRE and principal work closely together as a pastoral team with the pastors. The DRE acts as a consultant for the religion teachers in the school and tries to unify the in-school program and the out-of-school formal and informal programs.

The DRE relates to the pastor indirectly through the Board of Catholic Education, but directly in a faith community as a fellow minister of catechetics. Far from being a threat to the unique function of the ordained priest, the DRE serves as a specialist in catechetics who enables the pastor to serve more of the people more effectively.

THREE REASONS FOR HIRING A DRE

1) The DRE promotes TRE by programming for age levels and intra-level projects. The DRE can coordinate existing programs or help develop programs for groups that have no systematic catechesis. Besides formal structures, other types of learning situations can be offered, e.g., family clusters, or senior Catholic interest afternoons. The formal programs might include the Catholic elementary school religion departments, a lending resource center, pre-school, youth, and multi-level adult education. If there is more than one program, and these are staffed largely by volunteers, the DRE provides the continual motivation for continuity, creativity, and cooperation . . . "so that the entire content of the Christian message be continuously repeated for each generation in an idiom that each believer can understand" (TJD #18).

2) The DRE works toward TRE by integrating the substance of the programs with the three dimensions of Message, Community, and Service. These three categories are not isolated or new, but the emphasis represents a shift from content-centered catechesis to person-centered experiences of the community at work and the community at prayer. The social dimension requires the religious educator not only to **talk about** involvement in service, but actually to provide the opportunity for an experience of helping those in

need. Each program must strive to teach doctrine fully, foster community, and prepare students for Christian service (TJD #87). The DRE can incorporate the **doing** of service in each level so that the program taken as a whole reflects and expresses a giving, caring community.

3) The DRE is the unifying factor in the official structures to orchestrate religious education on the parish and diocesan levels. The DRE enables the Board to complete the circle of decision-making, program execution, evaluation, and goal setting. Through the DRE the board can effectively carry out its responsibility for Total Religious Education. The DRE is also the contact person with the Diocesan Department of Religious Education. The DRE can gather data and supply information to the diocesan office so that the diocesan programs will meet the needs of educators in the parish. The DRE can localize concepts fostered in the diocesan programs, e.g., Teacher Certification. The DRE can also help develop guidelines needed for specific issues, e.g., for parents of children making first penance. The DRE assists the Department of Religious Education to focus on needs and contribute to the thinking process that enables priorities to be established and carried out at the diocesan level. The Department of Religious Education can be effective in parishes that have a DRE because there is a single contact person professionally able to **do** religious education.

In summary, I think that a DRE is the strongest commitment to the challenge of Total Religious Education. The DRE promotes TRE by programming for all age levels. The DRE develops TRE by integrating the substance of the programs with the three dimensions of Community, Message, and Service. And finally, the DRE serves as the unifying factor that enables board and diocesan structures to be effective and efficient.

There may be other alternatives to DREs to accomplish TRE in the parish. I am aware of the difficulties and specific questions DREs present to parish boards. But my experience convinces me that things are happening that would not be happening without them.

This article first appeared in PACE in 1974. The author, SISTER MARY MARGARET FUNK, OSB, is director of the Department of Religious Education in the Office of Catholic Education of the Archdiocese of Indianapolis.

3
A Modest Vision

Yvette Nelson

The position of the coordinator is not that of a juggler. It isn't a question of keeping all of the educational balls in the air. It is more a question of formulating a vision and a precarious vision at that. It's the sort of vision which is completely aware that people think at opposite poles and that the tension that exists cannot be ignored, denied, or diluted. It is born of the realization that tension as tension is the working material from which a new creation emerges.

We religious education coordinators must be willing to ask, "What's it all about?" "Where are we going?" and "Why?" We must be willing within the community to formulate theories with the explicit knowledge that no program will ever be coterminus with the churches' educational task. In order to formulate the right questions and plan accordingly, one needs a sense of people. They are the ones who come into our lives—one by one. No matter what side they take on any issue, they are, not without anguish, bearing the brunt of the confusion. Each comes with her or his unique size and shape, with an infinite jumble of unlabelled fears, vested interests, and unspoken presuppositions. We ourselves are composed of many of these same jumbles. With a measure of compassion we can learn what happens in the ramblers, split levels, and one-room apartments of the world. We can come to these people with sensitivity and the full confidence that our Christian tradition is rich enough to support twenty-first century questions. We can operate with some confidence that the Spirit is wherever people gather in honesty to realize the future Church.

It is a humorous sort of thing really, a position reserved for clowns, not jugglers, people of star-stuff and clay, handling the present with compassion and sensitivity, while trying to realize a vision for the future. One small part of one place at one time. "One Circus, Three Rings, Forever and Ever, Hooray!"

QUESTIONS FOR REFLECTION

(1) "A chief struggle today is between people whose primary virtue is honesty and others whose primary virtue is responsibility"(Gabriel Moran). The fact that we are losing many gifted and talented people

in the field of religious education is a cause of concern. Many leave because of "honesty." They feel that if their convictions are at odds with the church structures, they have an obligation to leave. Others, however, who suffer the same tension feel an obligation to stay. They argue that we have a responsibility not to leave unsupported the people they work with. How do you feel about this question? (2) Do you agree with the author that "no program will ever be coterminus with the churches' educational task"? What do you think of Gabriel Moran's statement that the "Christian church structure almost precludes education"? (3) Would you agree that "telling the people the right thing to do is not part of the answer but part of the problem" (Gabriel Moran)? Why or why not?

This article first appeared in PACE in 1971. The author, YVETTE NELSON, has been a parish coordinator and has her M.A. in religious education from Webster College.

4
Speculations on the Direction of DREs

Gene Scapanski

Parish Directors (Coordinators) of Religious Education, like any other group of professionals in the twentieth century, are undergoing a certain evolution and diversification of roles.

While the role of parish Director has been rather successfully integrated into parish and diocesan structures in many areas, there is still, even in these areas, a certain ambiguity among church leaders and members as to the exact role and function of the DRE. We can take little comfort from a recent study of the role of Minister of Education in the Baptist Church which concludes that after sixty years that particular position still suffers from a significant gap in expectations and in clarity of definition among Baptist leaders. ["The Parish Minister of Education: An Examination of Roles," by Clifford Tharp, Jr. **Religious Education** 67 (1972) 289-297.]

If this ambiguity is present even in the best of parish situations, there are many other areas of the country where parish Directors do not yet even exist, or exist in name only as little more than principals of CCD programs.

The precariousness of the Director's role within the institutional Catholic church structure is certainly understandable when one remembers that church leadership has almost always been in the hands of clergy.

Six or eight years ago as a result of the Council, the appeal for quality religious education for all youth and adults began to be heard across the country. In response, the new position of DRE or parish coordinator came into existence. Because of the vastly different parish situations across the country, a certain diversity set into the field right from the beginning. In some cases (e.g., Detroit; Virginia) individual parishes moved very quickly to hire DREs who would work just within their parish. In other areas (e.g., Minneapolis/St. Paul, 1968-69; Scranton) DREs were often hired first to serve a cluster of two or more parishes.

Whether within a single parish or cluster of parishes, a next stage of evolution came as these Directors began to care for the multiple needs of contemporary Christians from pre-school to adulthood. At first, programs were little more than an extension of the CCD structure with added emphasis on adult education. Gradually, however, the inadequacy of this approach became apparent, and religious education became more than simply programs; it became a complete parish system with the many components integrated into the whole. In this system, everything that takes place within the parish, the very quality of communal life, takes on new educational importance. The liturgy, the budget, parish priorities and how they are set, collegiality, community concerns—all these teach, and teach more effectively than any "hour-a-week" program.

Within a year or two after the Director's arrival on the parish scene, he or she usually had developed the religious education ministry beyond the point where he or she could handle it alone. At this point, if the budget and parish leadership were amenable, additional staff personnel were added.

This was another benchmark for religious education. Up to this point, programs had proliferated within the parish to meet constantly emerging needs (e.g., marriage enrichment, sacramental preparation, family education, literacy programs, theology courses, retreats, etc.) but there was little time to develop in these programs the level of quality that they demanded. Much of the early discontent with parish Directors can be traced to this period of "isolation" in which individual Directors were the primary resource of their parish's total program.

A Diocesan Director in a large Eastern diocese once commented that he had oversold his pastors on the concept of hiring a DRE.

Pastors came to believe that obtaining a Director would solve all their educational problems. When this expectation wasn't met, disillusionment set in. What should have been done, the Diocesan Director admitted, was to set their goal on a team of parish religious educators right from the beginning. Then, even if they could not have afforded more than one immediately, they would have been less disillusioned when expectations could not be met.

In areas where teams have been formed, in the past few years, a whole new stage of specialization has begun. Like the field of medicine, the "general practitioners" of religious education are beginning to be replaced by at least some specialists. Certain religious educators are developing areas of expertise in pre-school, high school, sacramental preparation, adult education, liturgy, etc. The division of labor that is possible when educators work in teams allows individual Directors to spend more time on their specialty and bring about a higher level of quality than has been possible up to this time.

Even in areas where most parishes still have only one DRE there has been an increasing movement toward inter-parish co-operation over the past few years. In some dioceses this has taken the form of informal coffee hours monthly or quarterly to share programs and resources. Some DREs work together on a regular basis, providing area-wide teacher training, adult education, high school retreats and other programs which cross parish lines, maximizing the use of available talents and providing the kind of quality program that would be impossible on an individual basis.

Many of the DRE associations, which have been springing up across the country, have been an outgrowth of this kind of cooperation. In Virginia, DREs have been meeting and cooperating informally for more than five years. It was out of three such groups within the Diocese of Richmond that the idea germinated for a professional organization which would, in turn, further promote inter-parish cooperation and ministry, as well as service to the professional and spiritual needs of its members.

Another outgrowth of this specialization and team-ministry in religious education seems to be the number of independent religious education consulting groups that have appeared on the scene over the past two years. Previously, most religious educators, aside from publishing houses, were employed by parishes, schools or dioceses on a somewhat permanent basis. As the educational needs of parishes have become more complex, a market has developed for short-term, specialized services. These services are being performed by teams of specialists in religious education such as E.L.I. Asso-

ciates of Rockford, Illinois, Time Consultants, and other independent consulting groups in New York, Washington, and other major
cities.

It is interesting to speculate on the future of professional Directors of Religious Education within the Catholic Church. At the
present time there is certainly more job insecurity in parish work
than most professional lay men or women can tolerate. It simply is
not possible to sell a home and uproot the family each time the
pastor is changed, or working conditions become unbearable. Independent resource groups, such as those mentioned above, are
perhaps a partial response to the tenuousness of the present DRE
situation.

Parish religious education, over the past eight years, has developed through a series of evolutionary stages. This development
and the resulting diversity and specialization that have occurred
within the field, have been in response to two factors: (a) the complexity of the situations in which Directors serve; and (b) the tenuousness of the lay/religious leadership role within a traditionally
clerical church.

The role of DRE has hardly been fully integrated into the lifestyle of the Catholic Church at the present time. But it is certainly
the most deep-rooted and significant structural change within parish
life since the Council.

This article first appeared in PACE in 1972. The author, GENE SCAPANSKI, was
director of religious education at St. Ann's Church, Arlington, Virginia. Presently,
he directs the Center for Religious Education, College of St. Thomas, St. Paul,
Minnesota.

5

Redefining the Catechist's Role
in Parish Ministry

David D. Kasperek

This essay will attempt to develop the following thesis: **Today's
religious educator has a job description that has evolved over the**

past fifteen years to embrace virtually every aspect of pastoral ministry. As a result, religious educators are unable to fulfill their essential task—developing in believers a faith that is ever more "living, conscious, and active through the light of instruction." (The expressions "religious education" and "catechesis" are used here interchangeably. We are aware that for many professionals each of these words has distinct meanings. However, there is presently no consensus. Therefore, we are defining catechesis here as it was defined in the General Catechetical Directory—it is a form of Ministry of the Word "which is intended to make men's faith become living, conscious, and active, through the light of instruction" (GCD, #17)—and applying the same definition to religious education.)

AN ANALYSIS OF THE CAUSES FOR THE EVOLUTION OF THE RELIGIOUS EDUCATOR'S JOB DESCRIPTION

In the past fifteen years there have been many important influences on the formation of our understanding and practice of religious education. We will single out here several of those we judge to be the most significant within the context of our thesis.

A. **Catholic education is education of the whole person**. This tradition is a laudable ideal. It was developed primarily within the context of the Catholic school which sought—and rightly so—to embrace many dimensions: spiritual, moral, intellectual, emotional, physical, cultural, and social. As such, the Catholic school tried to carry out virtually every aspect of pastoral ministry. Within a school context this ideal is fairly realistic, for a total school program could supply all the services to be expected of a parish. However, during the last decade when school enrollments dropped and non-school religious education programs began to include more and more students, the non-school programs (CCD for example) at least unconsciously inherited this "whole person" concept. That is, both teachers and parents have at least unconsciously continued to judge non-school programs by the total education ideal appropriate for schools.

B. **Faith as a personal relationship**. This insight is one of the most important results of the renewal of the sixties. Basically, faith is seen as personal adherence to the Person of Jesus and the Father in the Spirit, a personal commitment demanding a considerable level of consciousness and maturity. As this insight was grasped by religious educators, they realized more fully that their task was more than the simple imparting of knowledge. They struggled to adapt their instruction to this more global understanding of faith. In practical terms, this meant adapting the message to a person's readiness. Indirectly, religious educators had to be concerned about the person's emotional development, self-concept, ability to trust, etc.— all important aspects of growing in a personal relationship to God.

While this more general development of the person is in fact the task of the parents, the parish, and society at large, religious educators in many places were the ones who consciously assumed the task. Consequently, they often had to take upon themselves the job of providing for such personal development as a first step in their actual task of religious education per se. The result was that the religious education program often took on the characteristics of a human relations workshop.

C. **The impact of personalism**. Parallel to the growing understanding of faith as a personal relationship was the virtual explosion of the philosophy of personalism. Within church circles, the one fed upon the other. Religious educators became even more aware of the processes of personal development as a prerequisite for a mature faith.

D. **Pre-evangelization, evangelization, catechesis.** The insights of the Bangkok Conference were basically intended for mission countries. However, here in the United States religious educators began to see many parallels between the need for pre-evangelization in a mission country and our own situation. While catechesis viewed as instruction demands that we respect principles of human development related to psychological readiness, cultural background, etc., pre-evangelization is much more global in terms of humanization. Too often religious educators failed to make that important distinction and, consequently, began to develop a philosophy that whatever awakens and nurtures a sense of the sacred is religious education (cf. the Metarie statement of the NCEA, 19).

This opened the door to developing "religious education programs" that ranged from folk singing groups to encounter weekends. The only rule became to find activities that interested youth and to sponsor them under the auspices of religious education. A review of the "electives" that have been offered under the title of religious studies in many high school programs gives some idea of just how all-embraching "religious education" has become.

E. **Renewed awareness of the Church's social apostolate**. At the same time our country experienced a group social concern in which the church participated. We've moved from desegregation movements through the peace movement into a more generic concern for "liberty and justice for all." These concerns become part of the religious educator's domain, not just in terms of theological or moral theories to be presented, but also in terms of initiating action programs as integral to the students' religious education.

F. **To Teach As Jesus Did.** The recent Pastoral, with its theme of "message, community, service," had the unintended effect of putting an imprimatur on these various aspects of the evolution of the religious educator's job. Though the document does deal with religious education from many points of view, in various ways it is very much a school document. Thus understood, the goals of message, community, and service are most applicable. However, outside the school setting it remains unrealistic to expect religious education programs which meet for only an hour or so once a week to embrace such a global concept. The whole parish must share that responsibility. Such non-school programs, unfortunately, have too often been saddled with the "message, community, service" ideal, thus officially making the religious educator responsible for total pastoral ministry to the students.

THE EFFECTS OF THE EVOLUTION OF THE RELIGIOUS EDUCATOR'S JOB

Each of the various events or influences described above is in its own right a sign of growth within the Church. But, as things have worked out, the religious educator's job has become so blurred that it blends into the work of all other ministries to the point where it is in danger of ceasing to be a distinct ministry within the Church. Schools that used to offer degrees in religious education now for the most part offer degrees in pastoral ministry. Social action programs initiated to provide a basis for religious education (e.g., establishing a center for the aged) become full-time tasks in themselves.

Religious educators join liturgy committees out of the conviction that good liturgy is essential to good religious education programs. They may end up spending most of their time in the liturgical ministry. Singing groups among youth, initially established to provide a kind of "pre-evangelization" or humanization, occupy a disproportionate amount of the teacher's time. Again it must be stressed that centers for the aged, youth groups, involvement in liturgy are all good and should be continued. The question raised, however, remains this: Are these the responsibilities of the religious educator or does responsibility for these forms of ministry lie with others? We will attempt to answer that question now.

IMPLICATIONS FOR THE FUTURE OF RELIGIOUS EDUCATION

We must be emphatic about one point at the outset. I have no intention of suggesting that we revert to the narrow concept of religious education as memorization of facts, truths, and obligations. This would be to ignore and negate all the invaluable insights gained in recent years about the nature of faith, the nature of the person and how a person grows in faith. So to see just what we are suggesting, it is necessary to look briefly at an often overlooked passage of the General Catechetical Directory. It is important enough to quote in full:

MINISTRY OF THE WORD IN THE CHURCH
17 The ministry of the word takes many forms, including catechesis, according to the different conditons under which it is practiced and the ends which it strives to achieve.

There is the form called evangelization, or missionary preaching. This has as its purpose the arousing of the beginnings of faith, so that men will adhere to the word of God.

Then there is the catechetical form, "which is intended to make men's faith become living, conscious, and active, through the light of instruction."

And then there is the liturgical form, within the setting of a liturgical celebration, especially that of the Eucharist (e.g., the homily).

Finally, there is the theological form, that is, the systematic treatment and the scientific investigation of the truths of faith.

For our purpose it is important to keep these forms distinct, since they are governed by their own laws. Nevertheless, in the concrete reality of the pastoral ministry, they are closely bound together.

Accordingly, all that has so far been said about the ministry of the word in general is to be applied also to catechesis.

CATECHESIS AND EVANGELIZATION
18 Catechesis proper presupposes a global adherence to Christ's

gospel as presented by the Church. Often, however, it is directed to men who, though they belong to the Church, have in fact never given a true personal adherence to the message of revelation.

This shows that, according to circumstances, evangelization can precede or accompany the work of catechesis proper. In every case, however, one must keep in mind that the element of conversion is always present in the dynamism of faith, and for that reason any form of catechesis must also perform the role of evangelization.

What must be stressed in the Directory's description of the Ministry of the Word is that catechesis is intended for believers. Granted, there is a dimension of continuing conversion in all catechesis and as such catechesis will always have such an evangelistic quality. But calling **believers** to continuing conversion within the context of a catechetics program is quite distinct from calling non-believers to initial belief—even if these persons "belong to the Church."

Until we are willing at least to ask just how many members in our parish are actually in need of formal evangelization rather than "continuing conversion," our catechesis will be expected to be all things to all persons.

The solution? It is suggested in the GCD when it emphasizes the close relationship between the four kinds of Ministry of the Word, implying that while kept distinct, they be carefully integrated in practice to form a kind of team ministry. In the same way the Ministry of the Word needs to be coordinated with the other ministries such as liturgy and social action. Too often, team ministry today means a group of persons working together in one ministry, as when a group becomes a religious education team in a parish. Our team ministry should mean the coordination of all the pastoral ministries, of which religious education is only one.

This coordination can only be accomplished, however, if we make a clear distinction between the nature and goals of the various forms of ministry, identify the persons or groups responsible for each of these forms of ministry, and jointly plan and coordinate the programs of each ministry.

For example, in the Green Bay Diocese all pastoral agencies are currently operating out of a set of common priorities and goals and have identified which agency most properly is responsible for achieving which goal. It is considered a sign of growth that, because liturgy has been given high priority, the religious education de-

partment has reduced its own budget and number of personnel so
the liturgy department can increase its own budget and staff.

Were this same kind of thing done on a parish level—defining
common parish goals and priorities based on an assessment of the
needs of parishioners—it might become quite clear that the ministries of evangelization, liturgy, and healing are much more needed
than the ministry of religious education. And it would also become
clear that the religious educator can't be expected **as religious educator** to incorporate the other ministries into a religious education
program.

Let's be clear on this point. Religious education is intended to
nurture the faith of believers primarily through the **light of instruction.** We are saying several things here. First, religious education is
only effective when presented to believers. It is not evangelization
per se even though it does call people to continuous conversion.
In concept and method, it presupposes a basic good will, a basic
motivation, and a basic adherence in faith to the person of Jesus.
By concept and in terms of its methods it is intended to nurture that
faith by building on that good will and motivation. It is not intended
either to provide the initial conversion or the initial motivation.
Second, religious education per se is not liturgy, it is not community building, it is not service to those in need. Religious education
is intended to **establish developing believers in an existing adult
community**, to aid them in participating intelligently in that community's liturgy and to enable them to become intelligently involved
in that community's service ministry to others. (By "establishing"
I mean aiding persons who have made an initial response to the call
of faith in order that their faith life will reach a level at which they
can assume full adult responsibilities within the church.) As such,
religious education presupposes that others are responsible for
nurturing the overall spiritual life of the community, providing it
with meaningful liturgy and directing its service ministry.

CONCLUSION

Based on the above, we feel it is safe to conclude that unless we
begin to limit the job of religious educator while we are bolstering
and improving the other forms of ministry, it's possible that in the
future there just won't be many religious **educators** around. Second,
religious education, while defined as instruction to believers, should
continue to recognize that good instruction must embrace the insights gained in the areas of personalism, psychological readiness

and experiential methodology. The **Green Bay Plan** is one such attempt to define instruction in this way while remaining religious education rather than pastoral ministry. Finally, if the religious educator is to narrow his or her scope of activities to instruction, even broadly interpreted, the other ministries must be developed at the same time. Otherwise, the "last state will be worse than the first."

QUESTIONS FOR REFLECTION

(1) How would you compare your definition of religious education with that of the author's? (2) In your situation, what functions does the job of religious educator include? What aspects of your job do you think refer specifically to religious education? Which, if any, do not? Would you change your role in any way if you could? How? (3) Do you agree with the author's conclusion that unless we begin to limit the job of religious education, there may not be any religious educators in the future?

This article first appeared in PACE in 1975. The author, REV. DAVID D. KASPEREK, was diocesan coordinator of religious education for the Diocese of Green Bay, Wisconsin. Presently, he is co-pastor of St. John the Evangelist Parish.

The Profession
of Religious Education

6
Questions for Religious Educators

Gabriel Moran

The most inclusive question one can ask here is: What is the purpose of religious education? If the purpose of a work is clear, one has some inkling of not only why the work is done but also who does it, what is involved, and how it proceeds. Unfortunately, the question of purpose is more complex than one might at first assume.

I must therefore clarify the question of purpose by breaking this question into two others: Why am I working in this field? Why does the institution of which I am part sponsor this work? These two questions will probably lead to a third: How much conflict can I bear from the contrast between my personal aims and the institution's purpose. These three questions imply an answer to two further questions I wish to ask here: Who (or what) is the enemy? What is the meaning of content in discussions about religious education?

1) Personal motivation. I am presuming in this context that the term "religious educator" refers to someone acting professionally or at least formally. One could argue legitimately that we are all religious educators, but I am assuming that a more restricted meaning is intended, namely, one who consciously and intentionally directs experience within a formal educational setting.

Why does anyone do it? Answers may include: I get paid for it. I enjoy it. It is nice work with long vacations. Or more likely: I wish to spread the Christian message. I want to help people. I wish to enable people to love God in Christ. The more exact question I am asking is: What do I hope will happen to the learners? And more precise still: What is the limit that I may rightfully intend as educator (as distinct from what I may generally hope will issue from education)? I think that all of us do have an answer to this question even if it has never been formulated. My own answer is: I directly aim at the learners' understanding better the religious elements in their lives and thereby choosing more freely what to do with their lives. I claim that this stated aim is neither vague nor anti-institutional, but it is carefully restricted. I would admit that my purpose, if achieved, does not necessarily produce practicing Christians. I would in fact think it likely that some people would get free enough to leave the church. I never advocate leaving the church; on the other hand, I also do not advocate staying in the church. I do not think advocacy is the task of educators unless one includes under advocacy the drive to state questions more precisely and the attempt to assimilate truth more completely.

2) Institutional purpose. The institution I speak of here is the Christian church and subsystems within the church. While personal purposes may vary a great deal, the institution's purpose is very well unified. The Christian church is interested in producing good, practicing church members. For this purpose it has a set of people, buildings, books, and language usually called in Protestant churches "Christian Education" and in the Catholic church "Catechetics." In sponsoring what it calls "education" the church has a self-serving purpose. The fact is understandable insofar as every institution has a vested interest in self-survival. However, the Christian church gets itself into acute problems by the exalted claims it makes for itself. What the institution mainly wants is conditioning, control, and conformity; what it passionately claims to want is education. The resulting conflict between the contemporary administrator and the competent teacher should not surprise anyone.

3) How much conflict? Every individual working in an institution has to face the question of disparity of aim between what he or she is attempting and what the institution in fact does. The preceding paragraph may seem like a harsh indictment of the Christian church, but similar or worse indictments can be made of other institutions. In any case there are always disparities. If one teaches religion in a secular university there is not the same conflict as in the church, but there is still likely to be a great difference between the individual's work and the institution's direction.

My question, therefore, is not whether there might be conflict but how much conflict can an individual tolerate while still working enthusiastically. My approach is not one of cynicism or pessimism but an appeal for realism on the part of teachers. Fewer religious educators would leave in disillusionment if they knew what they were getting into. One teacher cannot go counter to the purpose of a church-related school and at the same time expect no backlash. I do think that the Christian church can be changed theologically and organizationally to ameliorate (but not eliminate) educational conflicts. Such change is the work of generations and requires scholarship, dedication, and cool passion. It is not likely to come from bitter fights with parents, pastors, and principals.

4) Who is the enemy? The previous comments have implied the answer to who or what obstructs religious education. I think it is important to be clear to ourselves about this issue. I have indicated that I see the enemy in largely impersonal terms, that is, in the pattern of church organization and authority left over from centuries past. Our problems are not human beings, but the ecclesiastical claptrap and clericalized authority which is still so prominent in the liberal church.

5) What is the meaning of content? The wording of this question is important. I do not ask whether there should be content or how much content there should be, but what is the meaning of the word "content" in this context? In church discussions of education, "content" is a code word (like "busing" in another discussion). Obviously, anyone who has ever taught anything knows that a course has content. But people who talk about content are actually talking about something else. What they mean to say is that they want someone to convince children to accept as true the formulas of the Christian church. Ironically, therefore, the people who shout for more content are really calling for the elimination of educational content. Unfortunately, liberal opponents of this conservative demand seem to share the same educational premise, namely, that religious education is aimed at getting people to believe the Christian Scriptures and Christian doctrines.

The content of a course in religious education consists of religious questions which people have asked and all the answers that have been given. Doctrines play a more prominent part in Christian history than in most other religions, but even in Christianity the official formulas are a relatively small part of the phenomenon. The important question, however, is the way in which doctrines show up at all in religious education. Christian doctrines have a legitimate albeit a peripheral role in religious education insofar as they constitute data concerning how a group of people understood their religious life. The point of studying doctrines is not to get people to believe them but to get people to challenge all beliefs. By understanding what others have said and done, children and adults would come to their own religious expressions. In doing so they might find their religious life sufficiently consonant with the Christian organization of past and present that they would define themselves as members of the Christian church.

Education is always a threat to a religious organization; if trusted all the way education could be a help. "To teach beliefs" is practically a contradiction in terms; "to teach fewer (or better) beliefs" is to miss the point entirely. The question for a teacher is whether to indoctrinate or to teach. The question for the Christian church is whether it really favors education as much as it usually claims to.

This article first appeared in PACE in 1973. The author, GABRIEL MORAN, is also the author of many books, the most recent of which is **Education Toward Adulthood: Religion and Lifelong Learning** (Paulist). He is president of The Alternative, a mobile school of adult religious education, and associate professor of religious education at New York University, where he directs the doctoral program in religious education.

7

Three Views of Volunteer-Teaching

Gerard A. Pottebaum

INTRODUCTION

Presented here are three people's views on teaching religion. **View A** represents a father who was asked to teach a high school course on the sacraments, but refused. **View B** is from a mother who has been teaching since 1969 and continues to volunteer her services. **View C** comes from a mother who taught for two years, then stopped.

What these three people have written speaks for itself. They do not represent any scientific sampling. They comprise a range of dispositions which are easy to find in any parish today. They offer readers a set of viewpoints out of which they might begin to examine their own reasons for teaching, or not teaching, reasons for trying to teach, or reasons for avoiding this particular kind of work.

The following introduction to the three views is written to provide pertinent information which does not come through in the three persons' writings. It also provides the opportunity to make some observations and raise some questions which readers might find worth considering and discussing with their associates.

It should be noted first that these three views were written without consultation among the participants, although these three people do socialize more than infrequently. Each is presented unedited, with no attempt to turn their pen for propaganda in support of one position or another . . . except inquiry.

View A. The person who wrote View A was asked to write a letter in response to a parish coordinator's request for a teacher. He is an experienced college teacher. The reader might wonder why a person with the disposition he holds toward the church and sacraments would be considered as a possible religion teacher. Coordinators who filter out such people might take the occasion to examine whether or not their faculty is representative of a pluralistic community, or only of one segment of the various mentalities in their parish.

One might also observe of View A that the writer seems to be as recalcitrant about his position as are some of the people who hold offices in the institutional church about their positions. They would probably find him as faithless as he finds them incredible. These strange bedfellows offer coordinators a chance to examine what their standards are for judging faculty-volunteers.

View B. The person who wrote View B taught first in a small experimental program which was discontinued. Then she joined the faculty of a CCD program for over seven hundred children. "I am doing it very much out of a sense of duty," she writes. She has five children in CCD, enjoyed the benefits of efforts spent to train her, and feels obliged to pay back something of what she has been given. She reflects a rather tenuous position; when something more challenging comes along, she'll drop teaching. She communicates a sense of having fulfilled her obligation and is ready to move on to something that will help her to develop still more.

One wonders whether growth is one of the "occupational hazards" of teaching religion. It presents coordinators with the question of how to sustain the growth of faculty as the years pass, unless coordinators are happy with people who teach only so long as they are passing through a certain phase of development.

Reading between the lines of View B suggests that if there were a richer sense of community, of closer relationships than are possible in a large program with classes of from twenty to twenty-five students, an experience of growth might sustain itself for the people who are involved. But this calls for a model of structured religious education which has yet to be considered, as it suggests changes still too radical for these tired times.

View C. The person presenting View C taught first in a large program for two years. What she writes here reflects her thoughts on why she discontinued teaching at that time—early in the 1960s. Later she taught for five more years in an experimental program which was eventually discontinued. She is now a salaried faculty member at a parochial high school, and holds a master's degree in theology.

It might be worthwhile for parish coordinators to ask whether their religious education programs allow room for the kind of questioning, reflecting, and discussing which this person sought **outside** her involvement with organized religious education. She describes her reason for discontinuing in the program as a struggle "to relate my perceptions of reality to what I had been taught about God and life." When she had that worked out, she said she would feel ready to teach again.

What climate needs to be created within a program that will encourage people to stay on who find themselves moving into uncertainty and ambiguity? How can a program claim authenticity if it gathers together only those teachers who are sure?

Other observations might be made about these three views, not only from what they have said, but also from what they have not said. Also, each view can lead to a larger number of questions than are raised here. You are encouraged to turn your own stones, as you draw from these three views in examining with yourself and your associates whether what you're doing relates to how the Spirit is moving in unofficial ways in our times.

VIEW A

Dear Parish Coordinator:

I appreciate your invitation to participate in the CCD course on the sacraments. I could make time to teach, but I don't think it's a worthwhile commitment.

My reluctance to teach the sacraments is based partly on my perception of the sacraments and partly on my perception of the church which dominates the environment in which the sacraments exist. A few comments on each point may help.

In my opinion the sacraments of community and of love do not elicit a sense of community or love in most people—even those who are active in the rite themselves and not just passively present. There is more love, a greater sense of community and stronger motivation for service in a social evening spent in a friend's home than in any eucharist "celebration" whether that celebration is in a home, a parish or a cathedral.

I presume that the view that humans are born unclean and need to be washed (baptism) and the God's-scoreboard-and-lightning-bolt attitude (penance) approaches could be ignored. Nevertheless, it would be very difficult for me to convey a theme that baptism is a sign of welcome into a community, or that penance is a sign of responsibility and closeness to others in a community, when I don't see a group of people concerned about one another in the first place.

In my view, much of the institutional church's positions on marriage are based on a deep-rooted antisexual foundation and on a view of women as inferior. The Catholic college students with whom I deal daily have largely rejected what they see as the church's sick view of love and sexuality. Many of them laugh openly at attitudes toward marriage preached by celibates. Such students regard most pastors (and all bishops) as self-proclaimed arbiters of goodness in an area where they have no experience. And I agree. So it would be hard for me to teach the sacrament of marriage.

I'm sure my treatment of holy orders would be inadequate to the task. I feel there is no group of people who are less capable of doing their job than the present collection of Catholic clergy. In general, the best men have left and the mediocre have remained. The view that a special group of worship-leaders should be set aside — usually on a pedestal — is not relevant to the 1970s. Over the years the institutional church has fostered clerical supremacy. At the same time it has restrained individual liberty and responsibility for clerics (and religious, too) so that they find it difficult to become mature individuals. The question used to be "Why don't you become a priest?" Now it's "How can you justify staying in something as irrelevant as the priesthood?" So I couldn't be very enthusiastic over teaching that sacrament.

In my opinion the institutional church has blocked development of ways to translate aged rites of sacraments into something meaningful for the twentieth century. Pronouncements on marriage, directives that penance must precede first communion (only the clean can approach God!), commands to religious orders to maintain the styles and attitudes of the sixteenth century, castigation and censure of writers who dare to explore a new idea, and on and on. Perhaps the greatest evil of our time is the encyclical **Humani Generis**, wherein old men in Rome went against the overwhelming majority of medical, moral and psychological expertise and tried to prevent effective population control. How many times have Catholics heard that they must sacrifice to live by Christian principles? But precious few pastors or bishops have been willing to preach hard words on racial justice because the collection basket might be empty.

Those are my attitudes and most of them are negative. I'm sure I'd be a poor CCD instructor.

But why not stay and work for change? And why not start with CCD? I guess you make a judgment that some things are worth doing and some are not, a judgment that some institutions just can't be moved.

Sincerely yours,
(Signature)

The Town Agnostic

VIEW B

I first became a CCD teacher in 1969. My oldest child was six, and entering the program. I also had a four-year-old boy, and a set of two-year-old triplets at that time. I had taught high school professionally for about a year before the children began to arrive. By age twenty-seven, I had given birth to six (one died) children in less than four years! Since I had been a straight-A student in both high school and at Marquette University from which I received a Liberal Arts degree, I felt pretty stifled staying home and doing housework with "babytalk" companionship all day.

The first thing that came along, in which I was asked to become involved as a parent, was CCD. My baby-sitter was paid by the CCD office until the triplets were four and able to attend the nursery. More important, I was initially involved in an experimental family CCD program the first three years. Parents and teachers all met frequently both socially and for more serious religious discussion. My husband and I made some of our closest friends in our parish through this program. We also received many insights and good vibrations that truly strengthened our faith.

I had been raised in a Lutheran-Catholic home, taught both traditions, and chose my own to follow at age fifteen. I had no problem accepting the many modern ideas which had begun to permeate the Church in the 1960s. My own children attended three years of Montessori pre-school prior to entering a non-graded open-space public school. (My husband eventually changed jobs so we could stay in a community where these things were available.) I was just as interested in their religious training, and that it be as progressive. I was glad to be a part of the program, as a third grade teacher.

In the last two years, the experimental program was discontinued, and I have also become very involved in other activities (i.e., public school parent group, a "Catholic Junior League" type of organization, children's lessons and sports activities) as my children have become older.

My motivation for teaching CCD is now drastically different! I am doing it very much out of a sense of duty. I am very unimpressed with the quality of the school at our affluent parish, and do not plan to send my children there. I feel that since I have five in the CCD program, and since a little time and money was spent to train me in the experimental program, I have an obligation to teach, as long as I can find the time to prepare the lessons.

I took the sixth grade, which isn't too popular, and teach Old Testament history, which is pretty interesting. I am often rather appalled by the behavior of my students—most of whom are strangers to me now, as are their families. My classes are quite large—usually twenty to twenty-five, so we don't do a lot of unusual projects. I meet with the CCD Director and other sixth grade teachers a few times a year. We plan our lessons together, and have good texts.

One mother is a rare gem who just loves teaching Old Testament and will probably do it all her life. I'll probably soon find that other activities are more important and challenging, but I'll help out as long as I have the time.

I now feel more firmly than ever that a child learns real religious values at home, and that the main responsibility of communicating spiritual teachings lies with the parents, not the CCD teacher.

VIEW C

Catholic high school and college graduates of the late forties and the fifties who took the idea of Catholic action seriously often felt compelled to engage actively in some form of Church "apostolate" as they assumed their place in the adult community. Mainly on the parochial level, these works ranged from participation in the St. Vincent de Paul Society to teaching weekly CCD classes. They were taken up rather cheerfully by most, even though these people, at the same time, were mothering and fathering good-sized and growing families.

In my own case, there was a dual motivation, the one mentioned, as well as another: "From those to whom much has been given, much is expected in return." Seeing it, then, as a double duty, I volunteered as a catechist. It seemed the most appropriate thing for me; I love children and had an abiding interest in religion and theology.

My memories of teaching CCD are rather hazy; those years were punctuated by the arrival of our fifth and sixth children. Certain things do come to mind, such as the large white cards on which I had lettered words like "sanctifying grace" to be held up before the class, or the menu for a Paschal meal which I described and then handed out so that each student could take a copy home. Most of all, I recall an initial sense of needing some text to guide me.

My personal daily life was so busy and full that in order to do what I considered a "professional" job of teaching, I felt I needed a logical outline, a structured progression of ideas and materials to present. My own religious education had been along these lines. Even though I was taught that faith was really an assent to the person of Christ, this assent was always coupled with the need for an intellectual grasp of some certain religious truths. The more formally articulated those religious truths were, the more divorced they seemed to become from my own living experience. My daily life did not appear as reliable a guide for teaching religion as some outline against which I could check my "orthodoxy."

So much for my motives, rationale, and beginnings.

My classroom experience was not entirely unhappy; I enjoyed the children. More and more clearly, however, I saw a gap between what the text considered to be of primary importance in the religious development of children and what was live and real to my own children and my students and to me.

Of course, my growing discontent with this kind of teaching did not take place within a vacuum. My own personal religious perspective was evolving, my children were growing, the oldest was nine when the last one was born, the whole world seemed in conflict, Vatican II was summing up its sessions. Old answers formulated in times characterized by a static view of man and world no longer fit the kind of questions I was asking within myself.

I was struggling to relate my perceptions of reality to what I had been taught about God and life. I needed a time-out to question, read, reflect, and talk about all this. At the close of that school year I decided not to teach religion again until I had worked some of these matters out for myself. It seemed the honest thing to do.

This article first appeared in PACE in 1974. The author, GERARD A. POTTEBAUM, is a founder of The Tree House in Kettering, Ohio, an education consulting service and idea center for editorial, graphic arts, and environmental design talent. Pottebaum is also author of twenty books for children and three for adults. Most of his time is devoted to the further development of the learning environment, a description of which occurs in PACE 1.

8
"Total Religious Education"— A Realistic Approach

Mary Perkins Ryan

The approach I will describe in this paper might be called "realistic" since the question it raises is this: How do our programs help people relate their Christian faith to the whole of their lives, to all their activites as individuals and as members of the various communities and organizations to which they belong and to the roles which these memberships call upon and enable them to play?

The need for such an approach was first brought home to me by a booklet called **Listening to Laypeople: A Report**, compiled by Dr. Cameron Hall (Friendship Press), which describes an ecumenical all-lay project sponsored by the National Council of the Churches of Christ. With the help of trained "listeners" and local committees, the Project set up twenty-three lay groups in communities of different kinds (residential, occupational, and specialized, such as the academic community) across the country. These groups each spent from twelve to nineteen hours discussing the questions: What are the three most pressing problems in your community? What should the institutional church be doing to help you solve these problems? The reports from the groups all indicated that "lay people simply did not know how the institutional church could help them as men and women in their secular roles and jobs to solve the problems pressing in on them. They worship God in their churches, serve their churches as best they can in both their institutions and service projects. But they do not find, nor seem to expect, much inspiration or guidance from the church at the most crucial level of their lives— where they carry on their daily work and influence."

We used to be taught, in examining our consciences, to consider separately whether we had failed in our duties to God, to our neighbor, and to ourselves. Today it is perhaps more obvious than it used to be how interrelated are these areas of behavior: We cannot serve God unless we are trying to serve our neighbor and vice versa; we cannot serve our neighbor well unless we are trying to grow as persons, and so on. But serving our neighbor—fulfilling the command to love all our "neighbors" "in deed and in truth"—involves trying to do so, not only in person-to-person relationships, but in all the social roles we necessarily or voluntarily play. Consequently, religious education, if it is to be realistic, must help us bring the light of the gospel and the strength of Christian faith, hope, and love to bear upon all these roles, and not simply on church and family-related ones. And perhaps the reason why "religious education" still is considered mainly something for children is that we have not explicitly addressed a major part of it to adolescents' and adults' deepest and most real concerns.

Consider the following tentative (and necessarily overlapping) list of social roles which most ordinary Catholics have to play, or may play, or may feel called upon to play:

Church member
Worshipper
Contributor
Member of parish committee
Volunteer worker in some other capacity (teacher, lector, etc.)
Family member (husband, wife, child, relative, etc.)
Worker (at job, profession, occupation)
Consumer
Citizen (of local community, town, city, state, country, world)
Tax-payer
Contributor to causes and organizations
Volunteer worker for causes and organizations

All kinds of ecumenical and non-church-related movements and organizations exist, and are multiplying, which try to educate and involve people in carrying out all these roles (except, of course, those included in church membership) in such a way as to fight the "structured evils" in our society and to promote justice. There is obviously no point in trying to duplicate these efforts and organizations with Catholic ones. The task is rather to motivate Catholics to join in them or to initiate them locally where they do not exist, to bring the light of the gospel and Catholic tradition to bear on them, and to support those who become involved in them.

For example, it is certainly not the job of a church-sponsored program to tell people for whom to vote. But it is an essential aspect of "total religious education" to help Catholics realize why as Christians they should vote and first acquaint themselves with the issues and candidates so that they can vote to promote justice as much as possible in the given situation. It may also be part of the task to help them get such information or to equip them with the skills needed to do so.

Or again, it is not the job of church programs to tell people what they should or should not buy. But it is an essential aspect of "total religious education" to help church members realize the effect of their buying or not buying—especially if it is organized—on unjust labor and business practices, on our economy and that of the world, on ecology, and so on. It may be part of the task to assemble the evidence on both sides of a boycott situation, if other agencies have not already done so or if Catholic groups would study and weigh the information more seriously if it came from an authorized Catholic source (as was done by the Albany Diocese Lettuce and Grape Boycott Program). And again, it may be part of the task to equip people with the skills to organize consumer cooperatives, "alternative stores," and the like, if no other agency has done so.

All in all, there would seem to be four elements to be considered if we are to go about implementing this aspect of "total religious education": (1) How most effectively to help a given group of Catholics to realize what "loving their neighbor" involves in today's world; (2) How to help them realize that their Christian faith, hope, and love, and their individual and communal nourishment through the word of God, liturgical celebrations, and mutual support can help them carry out this difficult and complex vocation; (3) How to show them the way to exercise this love in and through a particular role, to gain the skills needed to do so, and to accomplish this most effectively in the particular situation; (4) How to provide them with the continued opportunities for growth "in Christ"—in celebrations, for instance—needed to motivate, encourage, and support them. This list is, obviously, an elaboration of the components "action-reflection," "prayer, study, and action," "observe, judge, and act" which have long since been recognized as essential to action-oriented groups, but I think that it is a more useful outline for the purpose of exploring the possibilities of the "realistic" approach to total religious education suggested in this article.

For example, the **Action for a Change** program of the Cleveland Diocese, designed to acquaint middle-class suburban Catholics with the problems of the poor in their area and to suggest a variety of opportunities for action to solve them, includes a theological component and also continuing support. So also does the **Action for Change** program of the Milwaukee Archdiocese, designed to involve participants in becoming aware of community problems affecting both middle-class and poor people, taking action to solve them, particularly through community organization, and equipping them with the skills needed to do so. Des Moines has developed a program called "An Experience in Renewal through Political Involvement" which includes prayer, study, and action—a program which other dioceses are adapting to their needs. The educational materials produced by the **Campaign for Human Development** are concerned with the rationale for Christian social action and the lifestyle appropriate to it, as well as with the specific work of funding, through the November collection, and projects designed to help poor groups help themselves.

Such programs are not usually conducted under the auspices of a religious education office or committee. Yet many authorities would consider them a paradigm for all religious education, feeling that action and involvement are essential aspects of any effective cathechesis.

However, since our growth in the love of God, of our neighbor, and of ourselves is so closely interconnected—as was said earlier—it would seem that programs concerned with increasing Christians' love of God and of themselves, and with interpersonal relationships are also essential aspects of "total religious education" in the sense proposed by this article, **if** such programs, at least implicitly, recognize and foster the kind of totality advocated here.

We might go quickly, then, through the main types of programs now being held under the auspices of religious education offices and committees to see how they might be oriented to contribute to this kind of "total religious education." At least eighty percent of those designated as forms of "adult religious education" are teacher-training programs and programs designed to help parents prepare their children for the sacraments and with their general "parenting." The theological aspect of both these kinds of programs could well bring out very explicitly God's will for human liberation from crippling spiritual, psychological, and socio-economic and political forces—God's will that every human person have "life in abundance" and God's "command invitation" to Christians to implement this will. Also the methods and skills used by the leaders of such programs and proposed to participants could be chosen to harmonize with and foster this theological outlook.

Teacher-training programs, then, could also suggest to participants the scope of their Christian responsibilities to their "secular" roles and explore with them how best, in teaching at the high school level, young people could be brought to reflect, in the perspective of Christian faith, on their present and future occupations and interests. Along the same lines, parents could be helped to become aware of their vocation to work for justice outside their homes as well as within them and to see that their lifestyles and how they carry out their roles as workers, consumers, citizens, volunteers all initmately affect their children's growth in Christ. I have not had the opportunity to examine carefully any of the most recent texts and other materials either on the elementary or secondary level. But my impression is that some of them are based, implicitly at least, on this kind of approach and would not be too difficult to adapt to it, so that children's religious education could be based on this same realistic approach.

A far fewer number of adult religious education courses are designed for the adult **as adults**. These range from courses in theology and Scripture to encounter-type sessions to help persons discover their own potentialities and relate to others. To these last should be added the various encounter movements for adolescents and for adults—Teen Encounter groups, Marriage Encounter groups, and others. All these, again, could be designed to foster participants' total religious education while achieving their particular objectives (What does Scripture have to say about God's concern for the poor and oppressed? About the use of your talents? What are you going to do about your potentialities when you have discovered them? How will you gain the courage and hope to break out of old ways of relating to people and take on new ones? . . .) We may hope that programs for adults as **adults** may develop and flourish, and perhaps they might do so if people could begin to find programs available—or be encouraged to plan them—to help them tackle their "secular" problems in a Christian fashion.

It should be said here that perhaps the area of greatest need is one which has mainly been approached indirectly, if at all: "How does one act as a Christian in one's daily work?" which raises the further questions, "What kinds of work are dehumanizing, harmful to other people and our earth? What kinds are worth doing?" Such questions will inevitably arise in connection with people's roles as consumers, and in connection with choices of jobs, occupations, professions. One offshoot of the Listening-to-Laypeople Project is an effort to train and support people to exercise influence for good from within the organizations they work for or the professions in which they are engaged (see **Lay Action,** by Cameron Hall, New York: Friendship Press, 1974) which is one aspect, but by no means the whole of this enormous problem with which theologians and religious educators and social-actionists must concern themselves.

Finally, what about the aspect of Christain living which should provide the inner dynamism for the whole process of total religious education—prayer and participation in liturgical celebrations? While prayer isn't necessarily or primarily **for** anything, it always implicitly contains the petition, "Your will be done," and it would seem an essential aspect of prayer-groups, Pentecostal and otherwise, and of movements such as the Cursillo, to increase their members' awareness of their obligations to work for justice and peace. On the parochial and diocesan levels, liturgical committees could cooperate closely with religious education and social action committees to provide, as effectively and appropriately as possible, the first and second and fourth of the elements listed earlier as essential to the "loving our neighbor" aspect of total religious education.

Here I have only tried to sketch out, in a "starting-from-where-we-are" fashion, the possibilities of this "realistic" approach to "total religious education." It needs much thought and development to become a reality in Catholics' personal and communal life, and to reach out to worldwide and not only local and national concerns. But I think that religious educators are in a privileged position to begin to advocate and implement this approach and to enlist the cooperation of their colleagues whose primary concern is prayer and liturgical worship or social action. Everyone is confused today as to what "religious education" includes. Since it is our primary concern and responsibility, perhaps we can begin to tell them. And I would suggest that one practical way to begin would be to redesign the next survey or questionnaire you send out to ascertain parishioners' needs and desires so as to include the kinds of questions with which the Listening-to-Laypeople groups wrestled: What are the primary problems in your area and your work? How might the parish, through its educational, social action and liturgical efforts, or others, help you deal with these problems **as Christians?**

This article first appeared in PACE in 1974. The author, MARY PERKINS RYAN, was executive editor of **The Living Light** and of **Focus on Adults . . . A Digest**, a publication of the Division of Religious Education of the U.S. Catholic Conference. Presently, she is editor of PACE. Her latest book is **We're All in This Together: Issues and Options in the Education of Catholics** (Holt, Rinehart & Winston).

The Profession of Ministry

9
From Ministries to Institutions to Ministries

James B. Dunning

There is some concern today about an indiscriminate use of the word "ministry," a use contrary to custom. One concern is that some use "ministry" so broadly that it eventually means nothing and becomes trivial. We are a bit startled when we hear someone proclaim, "Baking muffins for the church bazaar is my ministry"; or "Bartending is my ministry." (We must admit, however, that the author of the popular song, "Set 'Em Up, Joe," may be looking to his local bartender for serving and healing.)

Another concern, expressed in the late seventies by a group of long-time Chicago leaders in the lay apostolate, is that much talk of ministry has been limited exclusively to church-related actions. Historically ministry does refer to ministries in the Church. But to declare that all lay people by their baptism are called to ministry in the Church may seem, to some ears, to exclude lay people's primary call, which is to service in the world.

In view of these concerns, the bishops of West Germany note in their declaration on ministry that the service of lay people to the world does not constitute a ministry in the theological sense. Rev. James Coriden suggests that we should distinguish between ministry, which is a position of leadership in the Church—officially recognized in some way by the institutional Church—and Christian witness, to which all believers are called by baptism. This leads, however, to a further concern: over the centuries the clericalization of ministries, at least in the Roman Catholic tradition, has limited the term to ordained clerics.

In view of these issues, might it be better to expand the limits of the term "ministry," especially during this time after Vatican II when we are struggling to act upon wider images of Church as community and not just institution? Does the narrow, institutionalized definition of ministry perhaps stifle the Spirit who seems to be spreading gifts laterally with little attention to institutional forms? "Serving in a Ministerial Church," published by the National Federation of Priests' Councils (note: a group of clerics!), attempts to listen to this freedom of the Spirit. It declares: "Ministry is the activity of the Church as it is carried out by all members, at every level and under the inspiration of the Spirit."

Richard McBrien attempts to thread his way through the maze by speaking of ministry in the strict sense and in the broad sense:

> A ministry, in the strict theological sense, must be officially designated by the Church as a ministry.
>
> That doesn't mean that the pope or some Vatican congregation must explicitly approve. It means only that some specific Christian community recognizes it has a need, and then proceeds to select individuals who might be qualified to meet the need. . . . Ministry also has a wider, less technical meaning. It is a term which can apply to any act of Christian service. Ministry, in this broader sense, is making Christ, the Suffering Servant of God, present to the world, and especially to those in need. [Richard P. McBrien, "The New Call to Ministry," **St. Anthony's Messenger**, March, 1979, p. 22.]

TOP-DOWN OR BOTTOM-UP MINISTRIES

In previous articles I have adopted McBrien's broader use of the term "ministry." My concern, however, has gone beyond the niceties of precise theological language. My concern has been with our very image of God, Christ, and Church.

John Shea states that an image of Church as **institution**, with structures of belief, ritual, laws, and official ministries, will generally take a "top-down" approach which stresses the transcendence of God and his separation from human life, the divinity of Christ as his heavenly messenger, and a hierarchical Church of pope, bishops, and clergy who give the message **to the people.** This will separate the rulers from the ruled, the ministers from those ministered to— or, to use Johnny Carson's terms, the "givers from the givees." The danger is that, since pope and bishops and clerics are seen closest to God, they can begin to dictate downward the style of his Church and become isolated from the people. Then ministry may very easily be carried out on the terms of the clerics and not on the actual needs of the rest of the Church. We would be hard pressed to deny that most of us grew up in the top-down Church.

But when the Church is turned upside down (or, better, downside up), when God is seen as imaged and imminent in all his people, imaged in Jesus who is one with humankind, and imaged forever in all those touched by the Spirit of the Risen Christ, then we have a "bottom-up Church" in which ministries arise out of all the gifts spread out in all the people. Ministries become ministries **of the people.** Although not all will respond to the gifts of God, this situates ministries within the total giftedness of the community. We are back to a **community** image of Church in which ministries become not the private preserve of the few but the possible vocation of all. (John Shea, "Notes Toward a Theology of Ministry," **Chicago Studies,** Fall, 1978, pp. 325-326).

Gerard Egan describes this as a shift from a few designated ministers to a ministering congregation, and from vertical ministry, where the few deliver one-to-one services, to lateral ministry where the designated ministers support and challenge the entire community to minister to each other ("The Parish: Ministering Community and Community of Ministers," in **The Parish in Community and Ministry,** ed. by Evelyn Eaton Whitehead. New York: Paulist Press, 1978, pp. 73-90).

I have taken the position that this time in history may be much like those exciting New Testament times regarding emerging ministries. This has resulted in a broad use of the term "ministry." After many centuries of clericalization (although people went on ministering without Church permission or approval), we are now experiencing a new Pentecost launching people into the streets to share the Spirit's gifts. Ministries originally emerged out of the ebullient Pauline faith in the universality of the presence of Christ's Spirit: "There is a variety of gifts but always the same Spirit; there are all sorts of service to be done, but always the same Lord; working in all sorts of different ways in different people, it is the same God who is working in all of them" (1 Cor. 12:4-6). Talk about a "bottom-up Church"!

The process was hardly neat and tidy in Corinth. It will not be any more tidy today. In the process, some will claim the term "ministry" without precise theological sophistication. That is what I find in talking with people. People who just a few years ago scoffed at ministry as a term limited to Protestants are now claiming it as their own. At least some people like the term, and I have found that they resist the strict use by some theologians. It seems a bit arrogant to take the term away from them. The key issue is not the term but the image of God, Christ, and Church which is coming into being. I suggest we can, therefore, endure some birthpains as we struggle to find ways to talk about this new vision of Church and the new sense of responsibility which springs from our vision. I also suggest we can avoid trivializing the term by defining ministry through the **quality** of what is done (in Word, community-building, celebrating, and serving-healing), whether or not there is official institutional recognition.

I believe that our times offer some of the excitement of those early centuries which were marked by great flexibility and adaptation to people's needs when Christians sought ways to put their gifts in touch with those needs. Perhaps a brief foray into those times would encourage that same creativity and flexibility in us. Jaroslav Pelikan, the great Church historian, quotes the Russian writer, Berdyaev, in asserting that **traditions** are the dead faith of living people, and **Tradition** is the living faith of dead people. A look into history may free us from rigid traditions about ministries (and perhaps also about language concerning ministries) and release us for the living faith of Tradition which seeks ever new ways to share and express the Good News.

A LOOK INTO HISTORY

In the early Church one of those ways to share and express the Good News was the ministry of presbyter—but the functions of those presbyters were very different from those of contemporary priests. The 1941 ritual, with which many of today's priests were ordained, spoke of priesthood in terms of two powers—the power to offer sacrifice for the living and the dead, and the power to forgive sins. In the third century, these powers belonged only to the bishops. The crucial sentence regarding presbyters in the third century Ritual of Hypolytus read, "O God and Father of Our Lord Jesus Christ, look upon this thy servant and impart to him the spirit of grace and the gift of the presbyterate that he may be able to direct thy people with a pure heart." That's all.

Historian Gregory Dix states that the primitive Christian presbytery, like the Jewish from which it was developed, was a corporate, judicial, and administrative body with the bishop as its president. The presbyters at first had no liturgical function; the bishop was the great liturgist. By the fourth century, however, bishop and presbyter passed each other going in opposite directions. Due to the spread of Christianity and the increase of churches, the bishop became the administrator of a large territory and the presbyters became the liturgists for the local community.

Development, adapting to people's needs, flexibility—these are the qualities which mark the emergence of ministries in the early Church. Scripture scholar Eugene Maly writes in **The Priest and Sacred Scripture**, "We should not expect to find a clearly formulated definition of Christian ministry from the beginning, or at any single point in the development of New Testament revelation. Christian ministry was never 'frozen' in any one mold but continued to develop and to be adapted in the succeeding moments of history. Such development and adaptation continued even in the post-biblical age. . . . Development itself is canonical and therefore normative." The United States bishops' document, **Ministries in the Church: Study Text Three,** states: "It is doubtful that a single ecclesiastical office remains today in the same form as the New Testament Churches employed it."

That does not mean everything is up for grabs. I have suggested that ministries of Word, community-building, celebrating, and serving-healing are dimensions of biblical faith and that the faith of believers today will find new ways to personify that faith. But these ministries come first; then come the offices, institutions, and traditions which Christians find to express those ministries. This places the criteria for genuine ministry in the **quality** of what is being done and in the **faith** of the person doing it, rather than just in official recognition. If the person or community in its faith-commitment to the Lord is searching for ways to image God in Word, community-building, celebrating, and serving-healing, then it is enfleshing in ministries the Tradition of living faith of the people of God.

This broad view of ministry, then, means that all Christians are called to incarnate in their own way those four dimensions of ministry. Without using the word "ministry," Christians have done this for centuries. If this extended meaning of the term helps us view the entire Church as a ministerial people, if it helps de-clericalize ministry so that the gifts of the Spirit might be more widely shared, if it does not become trivial and just one more piece of jargon, then the Church will become more effectively a "we" rather than a "they"— those official ministers "over there" before whom "we" are merely passive receivers.

RECOGNITION OF MINISTRIES

With that in mind, if we do choose to commission, install, ordain, and officially recognize people as ministers, we need to keep several things in mind. First, such official recognition does not create ministry. The document on ministry by the National Federation of Priests' Councils states: "It is not that ministries exist because they are recognized by ordained ministers. It is because ministries exist that they should be recognized." Persons should be ordained priests or deacons because they are already ministering as priests and deacons. By ordination, the community should be saying to that person, "We rejoice in your gifts. You have been serving us well. We want to officially recognize your service so that you know we support you and to allow you more effectively to witness to what we all should be."

That brings up a second point. Official recognition through commissioning, installing, or ordaining should never relieve a community from the responsibilities of ministering but rather challenge others to live the gospel as effectively as the one being recognized. One American bishop has refused to ordain deacons until his diocese has training programs and installation rituals for other ministries which will be officially recognized by the diocese—an attempt to help people see that not only clerics are ministers. There may be good reason to compare our times with New Testament times. In those times, the fullness of time, Jesus as a layman shook up the institutions of the Jewish community and released the Spirit into all sorts of new gifts and ministries. After centuries of institutions which have become so clerical, perhaps we need to shake them up, let the ministries emerge in an atmosphere of freedom and not try to control them too quickly by official recognition. That might encourage more people to see themselves as ministers.

Finally, if we do recognize ministries especially for service in the Church, we need to remember that most Christians will minister **in the world** without official recognition. In **Religious Pilgrimage,** Jean Haldane writes:

> Behaviorally the institution's message is to equate church organization work with "real" lay ministry—and the rewards are for those who do this. . . . It ought to be possible to validate membership in the church and **ministry in the secular sector** as being bona fide lay ministry—an outreach of the church. . . . We do not have to manufacture programs of lay ministry—it is **already happening** as lay people interact with the world day by day.

In other essays, I have referred to ministers as story-tellers, prophets, educators, poets, lovers, parents, the poor, politicians, reminders and dreamers, listeners and proclaimers. These were attempts to move ministry beyond the church sanctuary—a step which might even move us to listen to our friendly neighborhood bartender!

I shall close with some imagery from Henri Nouwen. Nouwen says that each of us is like a huge rock, with walls and barriers that keep others out and keep us secure. But, year by year, God keeps carving away at that rock. We thought we knew what our marriage would be and something said, "No!" to that. We thought we knew what priesthood would be and something said, "No!" to that. We thought we knew what ministry was and something said, "No!" to that. We feel tired and frustrated, powerless, unable to change ourselves or others.

Then we discover one day that God's hand has created some empty space in that rock. We discover a cave hewn out of the stone. We find we have space to welcome people, people who also are so weary, so tired, so in need of a place to gather where they will not feel alone. They come in and say to us, "Oh, I see you too are a rock dweller. You have some empty space into which I might enter. You know what I have been going through, and you won't force your plans on me, manipulate me, or try to control me. You offer a place where I can be me."

God's carving hand seems especially to work in our days, both on us as individuals and on the entire Church. Once again, God is creating some empty space. We feel the pain of loss, because part of that emptiness is a loss of traditions—traditions about ministry which have been with us for centuries. There is also the joy of discovery, though, because in our emptiness we are forced back to Tradition— not just the forms and institutions but the living faith out of which ministries will emerge. That empty space leaves room for God to carve us more fully into his image. There is also room for God's people to come in and hear some Good News, experience new bonds of communication, rejoice, and celebrate because finally they have found someone who has room for them, and they feel the gentle touch of one who serves and heals. This is Christian ministry: allowing God to be present in us to form us in his image, and then welcoming his people into some sacred space where we can share the gifts of our God.

An earlier version of this article first appeared in PACE in 1978; this revised version is the eighth chapter in the author's newest work, **Ministries: Sharing God's Gifts** (Winona, MN: Saint Mary's Press, 1980). REV. JAMES B. DUNNING is currently executive director of the National Organization for Continuing Education of Roman Catholic Clergy as well as lecturer in theology at Catholic Theological Union in Chicago. He is also the author of the booklet, **Values in Conflict** (Pflaum).

10
Women in Church Ministries

Maria Harris

Ministry is a word and a concept that appears to be undergoing substantial change in today's church. Three meanings of ministry are easily distinguishable to most observers. At the heart of Christianity is the first, ministry as the "activity of the Church carried out by all members at every level and under the inspiration of the Spirit."[1] Next there are what might be called "church ministries," activities carried out **by** and **toward** church members by persons in parish and diocesan settings where such persons act in the name of the church and under its auspices. Finally, there is the ordained ministry, what is also referred to as "priestly ministry": where men receive the sacrament of Holy Orders and are consecrated by the church to act as its officials, especially in the role of Eucharistic celebrant.

The presence of more and more women (and of substantial numbers of men) in "church ministries"[2] is raising many questions about all three. I should like to begin by examining four cases which illustrate the factors leading to the formulation of such questions.

1) Susan Tunny, at thirty-two, is a former nun who has been a Parish Coordinator for four years. She is well known and well liked at St. Edmund's, a sprawling suburban parish with 1700 families, and enjoys particularly warm relationships with ninety volunteer teachers, who work with her in the parish religious education program. Susan is intellectually sharp, and has two master's degrees: one in education, which she completed while still a member of her religious order, the other in theology, earned over four summers at a large New England college. When asked what she likes best about her work at St. Edmund's, her ready answer is, "The people, and the community that has grown among them, especially in the religious education program."

2) Ann Hernandez, at forty-seven, is the mother of four teenage sons. She became involved in parish life at St. Rita's ten years ago, through a cursillo program that she admits "changed her life." From assisting the Rosary-Altar society in this small inner-city parish,

---

[1] National Federation of Priests' Councils, 1976.
[2] The fact that one must add words like "church" or "ordained" to ministry indicates that, taken alone, the word refers to the vocation of all Christians.

she went on to study theology in a weekly adult education group, and last year was elected to a second two-year term on the parish council. Besides her new found interest in theology, Ann has discovered in herself an organizational ability that her sons and husband always knew was there, but which she herself has only lately realized. When there is a need to "get something done" in St. Rita's, Ann is the one both clergy and parishioners call first.

3) Jane Walter, at twenty-two, is in her first year as a pastoral assistant to the parish team at Our Lady of Consolation, a rural midwestern parish. Jane graduated **magna cum laude** from State College a year ago, where she was deeply involved in a charismatic prayer group. She sees prayer as central to the life of any parish and has already formed eight prayer groups at Consolation. Most prayer group members are women, although there are a number of younger men, and one retired businessman who is a regular. Jane usually introduces herself by saying, "I am not now, never was, nor do I intend to be a nun," since most people appear to be surprised that a young woman should be so involved in the life of the church and not at the same time a member of a religious order.

4) Sister Louise Dunne, at sixty, has been Assistant Provincial of her order, a teacher at all levels from primary grades to graduate school, and principal of two high schools. She is the author of two textbooks on curriculum theory, has a Ph.D. in education, and is presently associate superintendent of schools in a far west diocese. A native Californian, she is a member of a National Task Force on the Ordination of Women.

Susan, Ann, Jane, and Louise, together with thousands of Catholic women throughout the United States, have a number of characteristics in common. All are deeply involved in parish and diocesan life—in church ministry. All have chosen to work with ecclesial organizations. All are bright, intelligent, and articulate. Susan and Jane tend to speak of their work within the church as "ministry," whereas Ann doesn't give it a special term, and Louise thinks of herself as an educator. Like many women in the church today, they tend to feel that they are stopped at a certain point, hampered in what they would like to do at the parish and diocesan levels, because they do not have an "office"; they are, like most women in the wider society, in middle management. And so they are wondering if, to be effective in the church they love, they should be working for the ordination of women to the diaconate and the priesthood. Louise is convinced they should; Ann, Susan, and Jane are not so sure.

The move toward the ordination of women in Catholic circles tends to center around the question, "Should women be ordained?" Asked that way, it is a difficult question to respond to adequately, since the only answers appear to be "yes" and "no," and the weight of theological opinion recently has the yes-es in the ascendancy. But the deeper question troubling the Susans, Anns, and Janes within the church is not whether women should be ordained, but what the nature of ordination is. They reflect on four characteristics that seem to separate the ordained from the rest of the people in the church: persons are ordained for life; ordained persons are not chosen by the community; ordination is prepared for at a special, separate place called a seminary, where the education is set apart from that of others in the church; ordination brings about a change in status, a conferral of what seems to be a kind of ontological reality whereby one "becomes" a priest, a different kind of human being who is now, somehow, a sacred person. These characteristics are not particularly appealing to many women—nor, for that matter, to many men, including many who are ordained. A great reversal would have to take place in the meaning of ordination to get the full support of the thousands of women actually involved in church ministry.

Interestingly, it is precisely because of their involvement in parochial life that they tend to feel this way. They are wondering whether persons called to engage in church ministry could not also be effective if they were selected (perhaps "ordained" **could** be the word) for a term—four or eight years at best—and chosen **from** the community to serve it in a particular way. When the persons were not doing church ministerial work, they would engage in the ordinary tasks of life as do all other persons—loving, working, engaging in the spiritual and corporal works of mercy as baptized Christians are called to do, having what St. Paul had, a "tentmaking ministry." They reflect further that their effectiveness in their own parishes is very much tied to the fact that the community has chosen them; Susan was invited to come to St. Edmund's by the parish, and a special ceremony was held installing her as DRE; Ann is in the key position she is because she is trusted by the community; Jane is part of each prayer group, and the natural leader in its paraliturgical activity. Even Louise is where she is at the diocesan level, not due to ordination, but because of the gifts, competence, and education she brings to her task. In addition, the education of all of these women, preparing them for the church ministries in which they now engage, was not set apart; it was an education in the midst of men and women like those who are their brother and sister parishioners.

Finally, none of these women is assigned a special state or status as a person. Instead, each is "in the midst of the community as one who serves"—**and** a member of the community. She is not seen as her role, but as the individual she is, and is thus free to play a number of roles: sister, counselor, friend, educator, church minister. Church ministry is neither her whole being nor her raison d'etre.

I am presenting these brief biographies here, and suggesting some of the questions they point to, because it seems to me that issues of parochial organization and church life are ineluctably tied to an understanding of ministry. To attempt to reflect upon ministry in the last part of this century in the United States, without seeing questions of parish and diocese as central to the reflection, may be compelling us to ask questions in too narrow a context. This is because speaking of ministry apart from the setting in which it takes place forces us to speak of it in a vacuum. Is it not, therefore, important that ministry be viewed in relationship to the central issues of ordination, organization, economics and community—more simply, the issues of authority, money and love? Is it not true that this kind of reflection is already well underway?

The presence of DREs, for example, has caused a rediscovery of community in innumerable parishes. What is interesting about communities within parishes as they are now emerging is their size. We are witnessing today the emergence of many smaller communities, sometimes of twenty or thirty persons (teachers, prayer groups), which come together to teach, to study, to pray. What might now be helpful could be a general move along the lines Bishop Borders has recently suggested in Baltimore. He has assigned each auxiliary bishop a particular geographical section of the diocese as his own province, and administrative decisions are now to be made in these smaller jurisdictions. The same pattern could be extended to parishes. Where there are large, unwieldy, and geographically and culturally diverse units, smaller units which are already with us—and others, as they came to be encouraged and formed—could be affirmed as autonomous. These "little churches" would, of course, interact with one another; in fact occasions could be planned where they came together for special celebrations. But for their ordinary, ongoing life, smaller communities within parishes would provide the setting where people would be able to come to know one another and to interact.

They would, of course, require liturgical celebrants. Would it be unthinkable for them to **choose** these ministers, designating certain members of the community to act as celebrants, as representatives and signs of unity for the community? Could not such choices be then ratified by the bishop? The difference would be that the person thus designated would only perform this role while acting for and with the community. While singing, writing checks, or doing the wash, she or he would be just like everyone else.

A second change that might take place in parishes would be in the handling of funds, a task not always thought of as a communal one. Women like Ann Hernandez, with her organizational skill, could easily become parish bursar, using the talent she has to "get things done" without the red tape associated with "granting permission." Full accounting could be made with reference to the way money was spent at parish and diocesan levels, but if this move were made in conjunction with that to smaller parish units, everyone could have some voice. As it is now, money questions are not generally the province of all in the community, but of a pastor and/or parish board. It would seem that openness in this area would create tremendous good will among people in parishes; it would also give them some concrete say in the disposal of money which is their own.

The public affirmation of the church ministry of persons like Jane Walter is another question facing present day parishes. Young unmarried women and men, deeply committed to the church, are often left out in the kinds of programs we now organize in parishes, geared as so many parishes are, to nuclear families and to the education of young children. If young persons like Jane could engage in ministerial roles without being looked on as financial risks (often the case) to a parish, the church might be taking a giant step toward reclaiming many of the young who have been disaffected by clericalism, noninvolvement in social questions, and the absence of genuine prayer life in many communities.

Finally, the presence in diocesan positions of persons like Louise Dunne might change the way parishes are related to the larger unit of the diocese. As things now stand, organizationally, diocesan agencies are on the top, speaking to and directing the smaller units underneath them, the parishes. At the same time, there is little interparish relationship, something which some diocesan agencies, built along more communal lines, are beginning to encourage. Women with gifts such as those which Louise brings to the diocesan level might be of assistance here, especially if they are women in religious orders. For, just as the governing bodies of religious orders are now becoming more oriented to serving their membership and encouraging intercommunity engagement, so too diocesan offices might more generally and consistently see service and vision as their main roles. Education and religious education offices in many dioceses are already in the lead here; given the kind of personnel they are now attracting, they could assist the redesigning of diocesan structure toward becoming more communal. The women of competence and religious dedication already in such positions could help to show the way.

Alfred North Whitehead once wrote, "There will be some fundamental assumptions which adherents of all the various systems within an epoch unconsciously presuppose. Such assumptions appear so obvious that people do not know what they are assuming because no other way of doing things has ever occurred to them." Our parish organization often seems that it is as it is because no other way of doing things has ever occurred to us. This is no longer true. The presence of women in parochial and diocesan ministry has already caused more change than many of us are willing to admit. They have caused some Roman Catholics to realize, with the emphasis on sacramentality that is our heritage from birth, that if we are a church, no one person needs to carry the full burden of ministry all of the time, while everyone is called to various forms of ministry some of the time. As women and men together, we are a priestly people, the Body of Christ, always engaged in healing, forgiving, feeding, burying, giving birth to, confirming and ordaining one another. And rising together as a community.

QUESTIONS FOR REFLECTION

(1) What advantages would you see in dividing parishes into smaller units? What disadvantages? (2) How is the question of authority in a parish or diocese related to the question of community? (3) What, if any, responsibility do parishioners have to challenge decisions in which they have not taken part? (4) Would you be willing to act as a liturgical celebrant if chosen by your community? Why or why not? (5) What are some ways young adults could be more involved in church ministries? (6) In what ways would you personally like the assistance of diocesan agencies? (7) Who is responsible for the nature and practice of the church?

This article first appeared in PACE in 1976. The author, MARIA HARRIS, was co-ordinator for DREs in the Diocese of Rockville Centre, New York. She is at present associate professor of religion and education at Andover Newton Theological School. Her most recent works are **The DRE Book: Questions and Strategies for Parish Personnel** (Paulist) and **Portrait of Ministry** (Paulist).

11
Ministries and "The Ministry"

Jeanette A. Lawrence

Ministry seems to be the "in" topic for many church discussions today. In this article, I will offer some reflections on the reasons for this widespread concern and suggest some guidelines for discussion to be found in the Christian Scriptures and conclusions that might be drawn from these for future action.

WHITHER MINISTRY? (Where are we going with our concept of ministry?)

In earlier days "the ministry" was seen as a noble profession with good standing in the community. The local priest, pastor, and rabbi had well-defined and recognized roles. This is no longer the case; the ministry has lost much of its former impact and appeal as a vocation. For example, a recent survey described in **Catholic Schools in a Declining Church**, by Andrew Greeley and colleagues, showed that a large number of Catholics no longer regard the priesthood as a choice vocation for their sons. The priest or minister seems to need to bolster his professional image now that other "helping agencies" are doing the kinds of jobs he used to do. No longer is he the back-yard marriage counselor, lawyer, or guidance officer. He seems to need to rejustify his role and even his existence. In some other countries, like the United Kingdom and Australia, churches are wondering how long they will be able to pay full-time clerical salaries, while numbers of middle-aged clerics are wondering how they can earn a basic salary and function as "worker priests."

At the same time we are witnessing the emergence of a fresh outcrop of new—or newly recognized—forms of ministry: "campus ministry," "youth ministry," "team ministry," "peer ministry," "pastoral ministry." We ought to stop and ask ourselves about the usefulness and validity of these new forms. Why has the idea of "ministry" caught on in this way? Who performs these ministries? How does one train for them? Actually it seems we should be asking what some of these forms mean. What **is** a "peer ministry" for instance? And how can there be a distinct category called "pastoral ministry"? Aren't all ministries "pastoral"?

WHENCE MINISTRY? (How did we get this way?)

In the early church, concepts were defined and clarified as the result of current practices, for example the creedal statement of the Council of Nicea. I feel that we are at such a pivotal point now. Current trends call for a re-assessment and re-affirmation of biblical teaching about "ministry." The present state of affairs appears to result from two movements. Some church leaders are anxious to "involve" the laity in church work for a variety of reasons including both economics and the need to "hang onto them."("Give them a job and responsibility and they'll stay in the fold.") Others promote lay involvement, not from fear of losing members, but from theological conviction. Some priests are giving up some of their own power and creating opportunities for their people to fulfill such biblical injunctions to all believers as, "You should carry each other's troubles and so fulfill the law of Christ" (Gal. 6:2) and "Each of you has special grace, so like good stewards responsible for all these different graces, put yourself at the service of others" (1 Pet. 4:11).

Again, committed lay people, with social and management skills for example, are also demanding more of themselves and their leaders. Aware, sensitive, and trained believers are not content to be decision-makers, planners, and active participants in other departments of their lives and simply "pew warmers" and contributors when they enter the church precincts. In particular, the women's ordination movement has made us all aware of our potential whether aspiring ordinand or not, female or male.

So it seems that we are at a time in the life of the church when we need to reexamine what we mean by "ministry." We need to demythologize or demystify the traditional concept which is now becoming so fuzzy and to reinstitute the New Testament meaning, which seems to imply that we should be thinking, not of "the ministry," but of many complementary ministries. I suggest that the idea of "ministries" (plural) is firmly anchored in the Scriptures' grassroots patterns and principles of mutual service. An examination of fundamentals is the way to direct our practices.

WHAT MINISTRIES AND WHO MINISTERS? (New Testament principles and patterns of ministries)

The concept of ministry as it is used in the New Testament is related to the idea of "service." In fact, the word used to set out the basic notions of ministry and service was that used for "waiting on tables" (**diaconia**): that is service—and menial service at that. In Acts 6 it is the word used for the ministry of Stephen and hence for our order of "deacon." He and his associates were to see to the distribution of food and goods to the Hellenistic widows in the church.

Our Lord Himself laid down the "service" of "ministry" principle as the **modus operandi** of the Kingdom. He used the word to describe his own ministry and also the Christian way of dealing with greatness among his followers. For "greatness and leadership" we are to substitute "service"—i.e., "ministry." At the Last Supper he asked, "Who is the greater; the one at table or the one who serves? The one at table surely? Yet here I am among you as the one who serves" (Luke 22:27). And, "No, anyone who wants to be great among you must be your servant, and anyone who wants to be first among you must be your slave, just as the Son of Man came not to be served but to serve and to give his life as a ransom for many" (Matt. 20:27, 28). Service is to be the activity that distinguishes those in the Kingdom. Jesus described some of the aspects of this mandatory task as giving food and shelter, befriending and visiting the prisoner and the sick, etc. (Matt. 25:42-44). Genuine believers are to see themselves as living in accordance with this kind of lifestyle. So the church should be organizing its opportunities along these lines, extended and filled out to meet today's complex needs.

Now, while the post-ascension church had designated leaders and leadership functions such as apostles, elders, prophets, it clearly held to the principle that each believer is a person who serves, with a ministry and contribution to make to the community good.

In 1 Corinthians 14, St. Paul, speaking of the gathering of the saints, that is the church service, says: "Let everyone be ready with a psalm, or a sermon, or a revelation, or ready to use his gift of tongues or to give an interpretation; but it must always be for the common good" (26). Obviously, the idea of "pew-warming audiences" was not part of his thinking. He expects every believer to be a participant and minister of some sort. Each one must find his or her service which will contribute to the edifying of the church.

Within God's economy, our gifts will vary, and no one should be expected to have them all. The New Testament doesn't know of the superman local priest having to do it all himself. The division of labor is neither haphazard nor a matter of shoving anybody into a vacant position. Ephesians 4 lists some of the functions in the church and clearly lays down the principle that exercising them is dependent on the divine endowment of the gifts necessary for each task. (This surely includes learning and training of abilities.) The gifts are for a good purpose. What purpose? So that the saints together "make a unity in the work of service, building up the body of Christ" (4:12).

Now, while we can see that some of these gifts need to be exercised institutionally and formally, others belong to a much more informal and spontaneous mode of expression. Ephesians 4 mentions apostles, evangelists, pastors, and teachers. Barnabas had a ministry of encouragement, others the gift of giving, and so on (See 1 Cor. 12-14). The endowment shapes the ministry.

What can we conclude for our situation today? Not that the present proliferation of ministries should be curbed, but rather encouraged. But we should be aware that not all gifts and vocations will have titles or job definitions. There should be room for expressive variety in mutuality.

In an age when social agencies are crying out for the establishment of informal support groups, we in the church have the basic guidelines and structures for living out the mutual life of faith—a life which essentially has the shape of a support group, a community. God has seen to it that we are each unique in our humanness and in the contributions we can make to each other. The local church is meant to be a network for the diffusion of mutual aid.

So, while the professional ministry may not be the way for all, or most, "ministering" is not an optional extra for the rest of us. It is our calling and our right.

WELL? . . . MINISTRY, HOW TO PROCEED? (the establishment of institutional and informal mutual ministries)

In the light of biblical concepts, we gain a new, yet fundamentally old perspective on the ministry of laity and priesthood alike. This view does not denigrate the priestly function, but rather sets it in a context of mutuality in service. Each believer should see himself or herself as a minister, serving according to divinely given and natural abilities and interests.

This means that the individual should be looking for ways of expressing his or her religious devotion in service which is both creative and suitable. In turning to our neighbors, or our people, we should do so with a sense of encouraging their development and their contribution. Who knows what different varieties of ministry we might discover with such an attitude? For example, the ministry of support can take many forms. Our age cries out for it, and Scripture anticipated that need, for what else is support but "carrying one another's burdens"? And what of giving? If viewed as ministry it too may take on a new aura—as it does in a particular way in the **Campaign for Human Development,** which funds projects that help people help themselves and one another. But the key is mutuality and the discovery and recognition of gifts.

An editorial last spring in an Australian Anglican magazine, **Southern Cross,** called for church people to see themselves as ministering to their clergy. In the next issue several irate clergymen responded. The idea was too threatening. One even asked "who has ever heard of the sheep looking after the shepherd?" I believe that such attitudes on both sides of the pulpit have deprived the church body of many resources and left many members unfulfilled and dissatisfied. In 1 Corinthians 12, St. Paul paints a gloomy picture of the malady of the body which has non-functioning or misfunctioning parts. The whole suffers. Some parts become over-exerted, others atrophied. I wonder if this is not at least a partial diagnosis of our present weakness and inertia—that parts are misused and the whole does not function harmoniously?

Yet hopeful signs are to be found. For example, one phase of the Bicentennial program of the Archdiocese of Seattle was called Ministries 76-81 "because the emerging theology of ministry suggests that every Christian is gifted and is called to share his or her gift, and that is ministry. A document published in 1976 by the National Federation of Priests' Councils states: 'Ministry, which realizes the mission of Jesus to the world, is the activity of the Church as it is carried out by all members, at every level and under the inspiration of the Spirit.'" (From **The Report of the Bicentennial Committee**.)

Perhaps the best image of this kind of church—the kind we need to create together today—is that it is a well-tuned, integrated orchestra, playing "a joyful song to the Lord."

This article first appeared in PACE in 1976. The author, JEANETTE LAWRENCE, is an ordained deaconess of the Church of England in Australia who did doctoral studies in educational psychology at the University of Minnesota.

12
Toward Clarifying the Meaning of Ministry

Dennis Geaney

Ministry is a confusing word. It means all things to all Catholics who take seriously the call of Jesus to discipleship. If you are selling ribbons at a Woolworth store and feel good about it, you may call it your ministry. Or you might be staying home and taking care of an elderly mother who otherwise would have to go to a nursing home. This you may designate as your ministry. Whether you push a broom or run a lathe, it is ministry if you say it is. At the other end of the spectrum, ministry is a role defined by others—e.g., lector, extraordinary minister of communion, pastoral associate. If you accept the role, you are a minister. Given these extremes, the confusion is obvious. Moreover one soon realizes that when everything is ministry, nothing is ministry.

There are two approaches to be taken to this confusion. One is to ignore it, the other is to work with it. The argument for ignoring the confusion is that it will untangle itself, if we give it time. Take basic words like "love" and "fidelity." These words are never rigidly defined. Every generation and every culture are always in the process of redefining them. However, in times of abrupt cultural change, as in the past two decades, the confusion can become chaos. The hippies loosened up the meaning of love and fidelity, leading to the sensitivity training of the late sixties, from which we have been swinging away in the past five years. The words "love" and "fidelity" are now richer because they have journeyed through another culture. They have endured and become stronger by being tested by open marriage, pre-marriage arrangements, the feminist movement, and a host of other movements that came into abrasive contact with both the gospel values of love and fidelity and our culture.

This Gamaliel approach to the word "ministry" would be to let it be. It will be redefined by osmosis. Church historians can describe what happened to the concept a century from now. The other approach, which I prefer, is to confront the ambiguity or confusion, to accept it as a challenge. By entering here into a linguistic dialogue with our culture, we can clarify our own vocation, become more intentional about our lives, work out our job descriptions with co-workers—thus reducing tension and increasing effectiveness—and contribute to the ongoing ecclesiological developments that better situate the church in our culture.

Like the words "love" and "fidelity," ministry can only be talked about contextually. A definition of ministry reveals the theology of the individual and the community. Its meaning is time-bound. Protestants began using the word "minister" during the Reformation as a way of describing all baptized believers as well as the person delegated to lead the Service of the Word. The minister was everybody and nobody. The elimination of priesthood only added to the confusion. Catholics, on the other hand, defended the sacrament to the point that all ministry became subsumed under priesthood. There was only one identifiable leadership role called priesthood which placed an indelible mark on the soul and demanded a celibate lifestyle and a distinctive garb. The ordination service can thus be more binding than a wedding ceremony which only bonds the couple until death does them part.

By extending ministry to all, Protestants devaluated it as currency, while Catholics drove it out of circulation by restricting it to an élite. Ministry was effectively dropped from the Catholic lexicon. What do we do? When a culture caricatures the word "love," we do not abandon it. We reinterpret it. However, we should look at the other side. Unlike the British language in which "ministry" has political and educational significance, it has almost no currency in the American English language outside of church circles. In Protestant circles it has never been able to bridge the gap between clergy and laity.

Yet the reasons for staying with the word "ministry" in developing the understandings of discipleship outweigh its linguistic weakness in our culture. Ministry has a rich biblical and apostolic tradition as the overarching biblical word including priesthood. The tradition restricts the word to people who are in some way identified with and responsible to a particular ecclesial community for a facet of church life. This does not mean that the woman who gives up a career in order to take care of her aging mother is not called to witness to the Kingdom. There is no higher vocation than living out Matthew 25. But what we are concerned with here is establishing order or roles in the community household.

While priesthood is a form of ministry, it adds **office** to the particular ministry roles that an individual priest may be fulfilling alongside ministers who are not ordained. **Office** is official rank in the leadership of the universal church. Through ordination the ordinand makes a public commitment to represent the universal church and be responsible in a special way to the diocesan and

universal church by a public promise of obedience to the hierarchical leadership. While he may preach from the same pulpit as a parishioner who is delegated by the community, teach on the same
schedule with lay teachers, and claim no special leadership role in a
staff meeting, as a minister he is both the same as a lay minister but
different because of the expectations of the official church leadership and the wider public. I am not trying to capture the theological
nuances of the differences here, but simply stating that the tensions
arising between priests and other ministers are deeply embedded in
the Old and New Testament shepherd/sheep images. While we
would be naive to expect perfect democracy with roles that are con-
stitutively different, we can work out viable forms of teamwork and
accountability if we have the maturity and the willingness to stay
with the struggle. We are defining ministers as people who are related to a particular community in relationship to specific roles,
which we term ministries. In this context, the concept of ministry
as a call needs to be explored. We also need to look at competency
as well as commission from the community. Finally we need to explore these aspects in relationship to roles in religious education.

The call has its analogue in the baptism of Jesus. It is first worked
out in the desert—which symbolizes our searching with God in soli-
tude to discern the direction in which he is leading us. The call is
not about what we do but who we are. It is not about my working as
a ribbon clerk but about my experiencing God's presence in this
work, his call to be present to the situation and to the people in the
store as his will, and how I am to bring about the Kingdom. The call
is experienced both in prayer and from the response of the people
we are called to serve. It is more than serving others. It is rooted in
our discernment of God's will for us.

If the call is to be minister in a specific ministry, one of the
tests of the call is our competency and/or our willingness to pursue
the required learning and skill training. The Diocese of Cleveland
has undertaken the task of outlining the measurable learnings and
skills required for competency in specific ministries. The Archdiocese of Baltimore has spent a number of years developing, through
a collegial process, the requirements for ministry to the sick. The
advantage of a diocese over a parish in undertaking such projects
is that, once a person is certified by the diocese as having the specific skills for the ministry, the person can move from one parish to
another. It also raises the consciousness of particular parishes and
does for most parishes what they are not equipped to do individually. While some may see it as a new bureaucracy, one must be
realistic about the wise use of resources. Indeed, without a well

developed network of interpersonal communications, it could become another pile of papers to be shuffled or another source of depression to overburdened administrators who were basically called to be pastors.

The minister must not only experience a personal call and be competent but also receive a commission from a community. Ministry in the sense that it is used in this piece implies that the task is given to particular people who speak and act in the name of the community in this area of its life. The minister is the bearer of the tradition and the carrier of the life of the community when that person is acting within the limits of the commission. There is a public character to ministry for which the bearer must assume responsibility, not simply as a professional, but in the total quality of one's life. We would like to believe not only that our Eucharistic ministers believe in the power of the Eucharist and have some understanding of the history of the Eucharist, but also the tenor of their lives reflects their aspirations to conform to the Gospel and make Jesus the center of their concerns. While no code of behavior need be outlined, if a person does not measure up as a Christian to the minimum expectations of the community, he or she will lose the charism necessary for ministry.

Besides the personal call, the person must be empowered by the community. Some people are recognized in their communities, not because they have been formally commissioned, but simply because they have performed the ministry long enough and well enough to have won their authority from the community week by week over the long haul. In a small community this method may indeed constitute adequate empowerment; but, in a parish that numbers hundreds or thousands, and with a turnover of twenty-five percent a year, we need commissioning rituals. The ritual may simply serve the same function as a clerical collar—that is, offer identification—but it may also be more like an ordination where the entire community is involved in affirmation, acceptance, and a pledge to be supportive of the newly commissioned minister.

Such a commissioning service has the advantage over ordination in that it does not presume a lifetime commitment which can lock a community into a lifelong endurance of incompetency. A person can be commissioned for a specific time. This element both allows for evaluation by a leadership committee and provides a graceful exodus for those who were commissioned but never fully accepted by the community. While a public ceremony demands a public commitment from both the individual and the community, the person is not truly a minister until it "takes," that is, until the living out of the ministry is a positive experience for all. This "taking" is not the result of a majority vote; rather it is an understanding that the person fits the community even though the community may be at times uncomfortable with her or his challenge.

In our brief experience with ministries in this decade we are finding that the roles of Eucharistic ministers and ministries to the sick are both defined and ritualized. Youth ministries, ministries to the engaged, as well as ministries to the divorced and separated are gradually taking shape. Here we are particularly concerned with the educational ministry.

We must first distinguish how we understand educational ministry—as a profession and as a ministry. The religious educator may see himself or herself as a professional resource person—that is, one whose role is "technical" rather than "pastoral." Indeed, when a parish or group hires a facilitator for a specific task, it is not calling the person to a parish ministry. The facilitator is to be of service to the parish ministers, not to be a minister of a gathered community. Obviously, then, the religious educator and the parish educational committee or staff need to dialogue about the expectations of the person who is joining the staff.

Many parishes expect that the religious educator be not only a professional educator but also a member of the worshipping community. In practice this means that if the person does not live within the parish boundaries, he or she must adopt it as his or her parish and be visible at Sunday and other parish services and events. On a practical level doing this (1) gives the parishioners an opportunity to meet and to share the core of parish life with fellow parishioners, (2) identifies for the entire parish the educator as a parish minister as well as a professional, and (3) helps the educator understand the symbol system of the parishioners from the interchanges that take place at public events.

While this dual role seems to add richness to the religious educational program, we need to look at its side effects. A religious educator is different from an associate pastor as a specialist is from a generalist. The educator structures time very differently from the pastor who sees his role more as a presence and overseer than as someone with one well-honed talent for a special group. Nevertheless, the clerical staff and parishioners may attempt to pressure the religious educator to enter other aspects of parish life, such as visitation, liturgy programming, and social action, just as they would an associate pastor—with the possible result that the educator could lose the special identity of educator, neglect professional development, and become burnt out from over-extension.

It seems that, unless expectations on both sides are presented thoroughly, disaster is being courted. Diverse theological and pastoral understandings can prove divisive unless they are first thoroughly discussed and then spelled out in the contract in specific behaviors—behaviors that can be evaluated and reinterpreted at times when the staff and parishioners have time enough to deal with the issues in depth.

If indeed the parish community contracts with people who are not only competent in their area of ministry but also anxious to be identified with the community as public ministers, we could begin to design liturgical services which express these mutual expectations. The service could then be a statement about many things besides the newly commissioned parish minister. It would be a statement about how the parish sees parish ministry. It would highlight a particular ministry and service of the parish. It would place a burden upon the one commissioned as does any public commitment. Finally, it would give an added authority to the newly authorized minister. We must repeat that being called to ministry cannot be used as an excuse for lack of professional competency and in-service training. With this caveat we can expect that, through the highlighting of the call by the commissioning to ministry, the local community will grow in Christ.

This article first appeared in PACE in 1980. The author, REV. DENNIS J. GEANEY, OSA, former director of Field Education at Catholic Theological Union in Chicago, is at present associate pastor at St. Victor, Calumet City, Illinois, and the author of **Emerging Lay Ministries**, recently published by Andrews & McNeel, Inc.

The Two Professions

13
The Professions of Church Education

Gabriel Moran

If one examines the history of the concept of profession, that history can be seen as something other than a straight line of progress. The modern profession, which embodies the nineteenth century ideal of the trained, knowledgeable, and well-paid man, is under attack today. Professions such as medicine and law are having to reconsider their histories and perhaps reappropriate some of the pre-modern meaning of professional.

If we grant that church education should be professionalized, what routes exist for it? I think there are two professions that can overlap in church education work. These two are not simply parallel professions; they reflect different stages of historical development. The first, which I will call "religious educator," is conceived in the model of a modern profession. The second, which I will call "church minister in education," has characteristics of a pre-modern form. My claim in this essay is that both professions can and should contribute to a post-modern form of church professionalization.

This position is in contrast to the attempt to make DRE a profession, exemplified by Dorothy Jean Furnish's **DRE/DCE: The History of a Profession** (United Methodist, 1976). This book contains some valuable information, but the author's equating the professionalization with the one job of DRE is illogical and self-defeating. The hope at the turn of the century was for a profession of religious education. By 1940 there were less than one thousand people, located exclusively in Protestant churches, who had the title of DRE. In the 1940s nearly all of these people changed their name to Director of Christian Education or Minister of Christian Education. Furnish fails to note the significance of this change—namely, that a profession of religious education had failed to come alive and therefore these thousand people turned to the existing profession: church ministry.

For many Protestants the last dozen years of Catholic interest in a "profession of DRE" are a case of **déjà vu**. Catholics, it is assumed, will soon discover that the profession does not exist and that the institutional obstacles to its creation are overwhelming. Catholics would be well advised to study both the Protestant experience of this century and the current crisis of contemporary professions. If the Catholic church is successfully to professionalize its education, the movement has to be wider than simply getting more DREs in the mold of the modern professional. The Catholic church should learn from its own history and attempt some new alliances in its educational work.

THE TWO PROFESSIONS

Anyone working in church education needs the support of some larger groups who are engaged in similar work. I will describe the two main forms of professionalization that affect church education.

1) **Religious Education.** The early twentieth century's hope of developing this profession remains largely unfulfilled, but the effort to realize a profession of religious education continues. This profession looks to other parts of education for guidance and support. Credentials are supplied by the university which certifies a knowledge of education and of religion. The salary expected by a religious educator in a parish would be comparable to that of teachers and administrators in school systems. This salary and the terms of work would be stated in a detailed contract.

2) **Church Ministry in Education.** This whole phrase is seldom used but it is the accurate description of many people in Protestant churches and Catholic parishes. These people look to the profession of ministry (or divinity) for support and for models of action. Credentials, if any, are supplied by a church body; the individual's personal religious life may be considered more important than the degrees he or she has. Instead of a legal contract there is a formal or informal sign of the community's approbation.

Both professions have drawbacks but both can be helpful. The problem today is that individuals may not be sure which one they are in. A parish can then get very confused about what it expects from "the professional." For example, most Catholic parishes have no experience in paying their professionals a high salary. A religious educator who asks to be paid a "professional salary" is likely to have a misunderstanding with the parish board over the meaning of that phrase.

The strength of religious education is that it could give the individual freedom of action and adequate recompense. The weakness is that the profession barely exists. But even were there thousands of well-trained religious educators, would parishes be ready for them and could parishes afford them? The strength of church ministry in education is that it clearly does exist; the local church provides outlet for the dedication of thousands of people. Some of them have Ph.D.'s, others have not finished elementary school— but that's not the decisive issue here. The weakness of this system is that it can be exploitative of good people, continuing the biases (especially sexual ones) that have been associated with church ministry for centuries.

I should note that the contrast of religious educator and church minister in education overlaps but is not identical with the division of clergy/religious order and laity. This latter contrast is now a source of some conflict in church education. The conflict cannot be quickly eliminated but it would help to use the two categories just described. The fact, for example, that someone is a nun should usually be irrelevant to hiring practices and salary. This suggestion might seem to worsen the financial plight of people called lay but eventually it would be to their benefit. The financial situation of parishes and dioceses would be clearer, and the chances for a more equitable sharing of resources would be increased.

There are people in religious orders who have become professional religious educators. Their larger salaries may corrupt them (or get them into trouble with the IRS) but that's generally not the business of their employer. On the other side, there are people who are called "lay" who are actually church professionals, that is, they are church ministers in education. We ought to acknowledge this fact with a consistent language. For example, the word lay does not belong in front of catechist. If someone has received approbation as catechist, then he or she is no longer a lay person in church ministry.

SUGGESTIONS FOR DEVELOPMENT FOR THE RELIGIOUS EDUCATOR

The religious educator needs to develop allies who are not part of the local church/parish. These professional supporters might include religious educators in other parishes, religion teachers in Catholic schools, people in Jewish and other Christian congregations, university and seminary faculties. The religious educator's mission is to bring educational critique to the existing church, including the very existence of parishes. For the sake of a greater church still being born the religious educator has to work with the church but sometimes seemingly against the church. This work inevitably includes accusations of heresy or disloyalty. Any religious educator in a parish needs both the temperament for some conflict and the support of professional colleagues beyond the parish.

Religious educator is not a church office. It is a profession free from many of the limitations of ecclesiastical structures. However, the freedom from the limits of the church also means that the profession's financial base cannot be solely the church. The religious educator has to realize that his/her full time job prospects are probably restricted to a small group of churches mostly in the suburbs. The other logical possibility is to create a contractual relationship with several rural parishes too small to support this kind of professional or with several urban parishes too poor to afford this service. I know of a few experiments in this alternate form but we need more data on the possibilities and pitfalls of such organization.

At present only a small number of Catholic parishes can support a professional religious educator; five percent would be a reasonable estimate. Many of the rest of us whose identity is religious educator find employment in high schools, seminaries, universities, and consulting firms. I do not think we can complacently settle into this arrangement. A comparison to the legal profession may be helpful here. At the end of Jethro Lieberman's **Crisis at the Bar** (Norton, 1978), he pinpoints the biggest problem as money. Many lawyers are grossly overpaid while most people cannot afford legal services. Lieberman proposes that every lawyer as a requirement to entering the profession devote time to working for those who have little money. He admits that his proposal is utopian but he thinks it should nonetheless be discussed. What he is actually doing is calling the attention of lawyers to a pre-modern meaning of professional (service to the community) which lawyers still support with their words if not with their cash.

I would suggest that professional religious educators should devote a period of years or a part of each year to people who have little money. For a religious educator in an affluent parish this could mean a contractual agreement which frees him or her for some hours a week. Such a contribution of time and skill would be a commitment by both the parish and its religious educator to the wider community who are less fortunate. Those of us who draw the high fees of universities and lecture platforms might also contribute some of our time to communities unable to afford a professional religious educator. I don't mean a grudging acceptance of some low-paying work but a public advertising that we are available for some of our working hours to those who can pay us only a nominal sum.

SUGGESTIONS FOR DEVELOPMENT FOR THE CHURCH MINISTER IN EDUCATION

The limitation on church minister in education is almost the opposite of what limits the religious educator. The latter profession hardly exists while the former is part of one of the oldest professions. The role of church minister in education cannot be improved solely by changing the job of the person now in education. The question at issue is the nature of minister and ministry in the Christian churches.

The professional I am now describing is usually in a local church/parish because that is where most Christian religious communities are to be found. The professional's loyalty is to the community and the community makes a wide variety of demands. The community may expect the professional to be available at all kinds of hours even though the service required may be simple and unspecialized (supervising a gym, serving meals). The community in turn should support the professional in a variety of ways.

The rewards for this kind of work are not mainly financial. While money is one legitimate sign of support, the church community has a duty to resist the reduction of all values to market terms. The greater reward here is the recognition that one is using God-given talents to help others in educational ways. The main educational effort is to provide people with the experience of belonging to a Christian community. The aim is to develop a community of communities, each with a competence that could be called professional.

Some of the competent and dedicated people who do church work are unpaid volunteers. Others of its professionals are paid but not usually in straight salary. The eighteenth century church provided land to the minister so that he could farm. Today the community may provide housing which, it should be carefully noted, is a symbol of the professional's relation to the community. Other supports (e.g., a car) are less clear symbolically but they are part of an intricate relation of personal life and professional work. Anyone entering this profession should be aware of the meaning of this financial arrangement. Especially if the person is head of a household, he or she would do well to discuss with his or her family the restrictions built into this profession.

A written agreement can be helpful here but it does not have to be a legal contract. The need is to avoid misunderstandings by a statement of minimum expectations for professional and community. If there isn't trust between these parties a detailed contract will not substitute for it. Furthermore, a current misconception assumes that the mark of a professional is the contract. Lieberman

appeals to an older and richer meaning when he writes: "Professionalism consists in doing right though the sanctions of law are
absent." I would like to be protected in my work from exploitation
and misunderstandings; nevertheless, I would also like to use my
imagination to re-create the job into something neither I nor my
hirer can forsee.

CONCLUSION

A Catholic parish isn't to be modeled on the modern university or
the nation state. We don't need a bigger professional class to serve
more consumers. Minister and ministry should be moving in the
direction of encompassing everyone who wishes to devote time,
talent, and training to the church. Note that the current interest
in many professions to get "paraprofessionals" for the routine work
may not be a move in the same direction. We don't need an inter-
mediary class so that the professionals can become more esoteric
and protected. A church community should consist of people with
a variety of skills (some without credentials from a university)
trained to varying degrees. Every parish member should be able to
share in the professional work of the church.

The typical Catholic parish, therefore, should have dozens,
hundreds, or thousands of "professional ministers." That means a
considerable shift in church language and in parish resources. A
large part of parish money should be used for educating hundreds
of the parish's ministers. Would that mean a big cut in pay for the
one, two, or three now called ministers? Perhaps. But Catholics in
this country have been remarkably generous with money for the
church. In many places this generosity is not being tapped today
for educational programs that the community can recognize as
worthwhile.

The parish should be a reminder to the wider society that its
problems can be solved only if people care for each other at the
personal, familial, and communal level. If I am able to care, to
reconcile, to teach, to counsel, to guide a discussion, I can be part
of the church's professional ministry of education. Parishes usually
do need someone to coordinate or direct the educational resources
of the community; hence a title to that effect can appropriately
apply to one of the church's ministers. Parishes can also use the
challenge of religious educators who respect current church structure but do not assume it is forever fixed. With the help of people
in both professions the people who are the professing Christians

can give witness to the world of a renewed church. The post-modern form of professionalization draws upon the church's past, accepts the history of modern times, and creates for the future era communities of teaching and service.

(companion essay follows)

14
Parish Models of Education

Gabriel Moran

In a companion essay, I distinguished two professions which can overlap in the church's educational work. Here I would like to describe how this convergence of the two professions might operate in large, small, and middle-sized parishes.

We first have to recognize that the word "parish" does not always refer to the same kind of organization. "Parish" may mean a complex modern organization of thousands of people, or it can mean a few dozen people with a minimum of organization. These two ends of the spectrum have some things in common which set them off from the intermediate-sized parish. Just as a large, old city in many ways resembles a rural village more than it resembles its neighboring suburbs, so also the "super parish" and the "mini parish" have much that they share. The intermediate-sized parish is where the greatest confusion lies today, and I will address that question last.

If one is trying to describe the future parish, the place to start is with super parishes. If they are well organized they will have many mini parishes within them. The intermediate-sized parish can learn from both the large and small parishes. Eventually it will have to move in both directions; that is, on its own or by amalgamation, it will have to develop more central organization but at the same time cultivate mini parishes as the basic organizing unit. The policy of simply dividing a parish of 1,500 households into two of 750 may seem logical to a bureaucracy but it makes no sense in communal or educational terms.

I) THE SUPER PARISH

What can be imagined for a large and well-organized parish? There would be a group or team of ministers who direct the work of the parish in areas of liturgy, social service, and education. The group would be accountable to a council or board elected with the help of the best available political process and means of communication. The inner group of six or eight ministers would divide the work in a way that fits the specific needs of the parish.

One of the people might be called the minister of education. The job would be twofold. Internal to the group, he or she would monitor the language, imagery, and direction of the ministerial team to prevent its becoming a bureaucratic élite. Externally, the task would be to involve as many people as possible in the educational ministry of the church. The question is not how to fill eight teaching slots in the church school but how to involve adults and children in hundreds of ways. One person cannot do all that needs doing, but one person can imagine and/or coordinate the efforts. The job might best be done, not by a scholar, but by someone who has roots in the parish and is already an organizer. The job ought to have a recompense, but the visible support of the parish might be as valuable as money to such a person.

In addition to this core of ministers, a super parish should be able to hire at least one and preferably two religious educators. While they may in practice function in close relationship with the parish ministers, they are employed on a different basis and for a different purpose. They bring to the parish a supra-parochial vision and the specialized training of the university. Education includes many kinds of personal growth—in the family, on the job, and through leisure. However, parish religious educators are particularly concerned with schooling, that is, the learning from books, courses, and systematic study. Occasionally they would run courses for the parish at large. More often they would teach the teachers of the parish (most parents and many other adults). They might engage in their professional work only twelve to eighteen hours a week, but they would be delivering an invaluable resource to the parish.

These modern professionals should be paid the going rate for such professional service. Many existing parishes have the money for one, two, or more religious educators, but parishes are still confused about what a religious educator is. Note that the existence of a parish school should be an ally rather than a foe in developing the category of "professional religious educator." People know that to maintain a school building and a faculty requires large amounts of money. If a parish is committed to a school, the argument can be made that comparable professional service should be available to the rest of the parish. If a school does not exist or is closing, professional religious educator(s) can be seen as a bargain. In any case, some respected voices in the parish ought to argue for a religious education budget of many tens of thousands of dollars.

II) THE MINI PARISH

The very small parish is likely to be found (a) in rural towns, (b) in depressed urban areas, and/or (c) in experiments of communities found in various geographical areas. In each case the mini parish might learn something from the super parish, and in turn a well-organized super parish should cultivate the mini parish. In the mini parish, the organizational question appears to be simple, but key roles still function. There is likely to be only one paid position, and even that one may not be a full-time job. One person cannot do everything, and so his or her main task is to get many people involved in the parish's work. This person, who is probably called the pastor, is also functioning as the minister of education. Instead of electing a parish council, it makes more sense for the entire parish to be the board of directors.

One drawback to this informal kind of parish is the lack of a professional religious educator. The mini parish cannot support one. Two ways of adapting are possible:

a) The mini parish might be connected to a super parish that would release one of its religious educators to work with the mini parish. The connection would be especially appropriate where the small parish is urban and poor. The arrangement might free the religious educator for as much as a full day a week or for just an evening a month; the important thing is to start the relationship.

b) The pastor/minister of education might work out a variety of relationships with local colleges, other churches, libraries, businesses, and anyone else who could be of educational help. Many services are free, but people may not know of them. For additional help in religious education, the mini parish might judiciously spend its money for outside consultants.

III) THE INTERMEDIATE PARISH

The confusions of church life and especially religious education show up in the medium-sized parish which is not large enough to be an efficient organization and not small enough to be a community inviting everyone's participation. In the light of the discussion of large and small parishes, some clarification might be brought to the confusions of the medium-sized parish.

The person hired to be DRE/Coordinator in such a parish is liable to face this situation: (a) be expected to do the two different jobs I have described as church minister of education and religious educator; (b) be paid less than professional educators but be criticized for being more expensive than other church ministers; (c) be expected to educate the whole parish but have neither the resources nor the freedom that the process of education requires. A person who is taking this job should know exactly what crossfire he or she is walking into.

People who become DRE/Coordinators in medium-sized parishes are sometimes confused about their own demands. If the person wants everything spelled out in a contract, then he or she cannot logically complain of being treated like an employee rather than a member of the community. The choice isn't always exclusive but the DRE/Coordinator has to choose which of the two roles to emphasize. If he or she wishes to be an integral element of the parish ministerial team, then the important thing is building trust and getting an oral understanding with the parish board and other parish ministers. The written agreement becomes brief, secondary, and not really a contract for services.

If, by choice or necessity, one wishes to be a religious educator in the modern mold, that fact should be made crystal clear to board, pastor, and everyone else concerned. The limits of the parish demands should be precisely stated, but the other side should also be clear—namely, that the professional religious educator does not expect the parish to be a constant souce of community experience and support. The DRE/Coordinator here should expect to be treated as neither more nor less than a paid professional. The work can be friendly, enjoyable, and stimulating, but the parish's main sign of support is the paying of a living wage.

Many medium-sized parishes are hiring a DRE/Coordinator and working through some inevitable confusion and conflict. The process can represent real progress in the Catholic Church. However, some parishes advertising in the press for a DRE/Coordinator should be advised that they don't know what they are doing. Unless a parish can offer a living wage (something above the U.S. government's poverty level for that area), it should probably go another route. This proposal may seem to reduce employment opportunities for educators in search of jobs, but I see little advantage in people getting caught in intolerable situations because of being paid scandalously low wages.

I would emphasize that there are alternate routes for a parish to go. Improving (or professionalizing) church education is not necessarily accomplished by hiring a DRE/Coordinator. Should the parish have only $6,000 for this purpose, there are other ways to spend the money than to get one overworked and underpaid person to do the whole job. Why not bring in, on a temporary basis, someone whose aim would be to organize the existing resources of the parish? For a modest fee a professional religious educator might be found who would be a regular consultant to the parish but not a full-time employee. Many university or seminary faculty members would be glad to have the work.

Another worthwhile investment for a parish is educational grants for parish members. Some equitable system has to be devised for distributing the money, but that is not too difficult to do. If a parish is committed to $6,000 worth of religious education, why can't it be in grants of $100 to $300 to the most astute and alive people in the parish? Some of the best students I meet in institutes and graduate programs are there on such diocesan and parish grants. The tragedy is that there are not thousands more of them. At the end of five years the parish could have, not a continuing struggle to hold on to a DRE/Coordinator, but a dozen or more of its own professionally trained religious educators.

In summary, the U.S. Catholic Church should not be thinking of trying to professionalize education by hiring one DRE/Coordinator for each parish. The two relevant questions are (1) How do we organize whatever resources already exist in a parish so that most parishioners can be part of the professional ministry of education? (2) How do we bring the critical thinking of the academic world to bear on the parish? The DRE/Coordinator can be part of the answer to both questions, but hiring a DRE/Coordinator may not be the appropriate response in many situations.

The picture for the very large and very small parishes is clear. For the medium-sized parish, one can only advise: (1) study large and small parishes; (2) take stock of the parish resources and needs; (3) use available money for imaginative and temporary programs in religious education until a larger investment has broad parish support; (4) hire one or more professional religious educators when a good salary can be paid and when parish leaders know exactly what services they need.

This and the preceding article first appeared in PACE in 1978. The author, GABRIEL MORAN, presently directs the doctoral program in religious education at New York University, where he is associate professor of religious education. His new book is **Education Toward Adulthood: Religion and Lifelong Learning** (Paulist).

(Some of) The Many Roles of the DRE:
Theologian
Executive
Administrator
Spiritual Director

15
What Role Do You Fill?

Kenneth R. Mitchell

After studying the systems in which people work—mostly churches, but also hospitals and businesses—I've been driven to the conclusion that nobody really knows what his or her job is. Oh, yes, we have our job titles and two pages of "duties" to go with them. We even have mental lists of things we're expected to do, things that didn't get written into the job descriptions. But that doesn't tell the whole story. In fact, we take part in a conspiracy never to tell the whole story, and never to let it get told.

For example, three years ago, a subtle but drastic change took place in our office. We had a staff secretary named Gloria, who left us to move to California. Her job title and description: staff secretary, to answer telephones, take dictation, type, and maintain files. As far as our nine hundred-employee organization cared, that was what was expected of her. Within our department, we'd also assigned Gloria some jobs that needed to be done, jobs not assigned by The Menninger Foundation. She was a secretary to a particular person; she sold stamps and got the mail, and she organized our workshops.

So far so good. But Gloria did something else, too. Almost every day, she brought in a joke or a cartoon from a magazine (it was almost always a joke about counselors or ministers) and pinned it to the bulletin board in her office. Gloria's "joke board" became a gathering place in the office. Everybody managed to see it at least once a day.

After Gloria left, I was free to hire a new staff secretary. I assigned her to the post-office function, and she became the secretary for one of our staff. Martee was cheerful, outgoing, competent, and efficient. But she didn't keep up the joke board, **and that was a job to which I couldn't assign her.**

In every human system, we fill three kinds of roles. There are **formal roles**, which consist of job titles and descriptions, publicly known to the whole organization, and about which the organization cares. There are **informal roles**, assigned by the local person in authority, about which the total organization seems not to care much. These are not written into a job description, but they are arranged and agreed to. Finally, there are **tacit roles**. These are seldom if ever discussed, and if the worker is not interested in them, they'll probably not be assigned to someone else. (Of course not, if we don't talk about them!) But their presence or absence makes a very great difference in the organization.

Formal roles in church life can usually be identified by a noun, and the noun usually corresponds to a job title: Pastor, Director of Christian Education; Custodian; Church Secretary; Priest; Nun. You can usually fit formal roles into the following sentence: "If we lose our _____ , we can get another one."

Informal roles are identified in much the same way, although a phrase or sentence may be necessary: "Father Hoffnecker's secretary." "The guy who helps the scoutmaster." "Whoever locks up around here." Both formal and informal roles have the flavor given to them by the purposes of the organization, and the nature of its business.

When we name tacit roles, they often have a peculiar look to them: Morale-builder; Cake-baker for birthdays; Joke-board-keeper; Resident nitwit. And if we lose our (**fill in tacit role**) , there's no way in the world except by luck or the grace of God that we can get another. But every system **needs** to have certain tacit roles filled, and since on the one hand it needs them and on the other hand can't assign them, the organization feels a peculiar discomfort when they are unfilled, and often—tacitly, of course—pressures someone to fill them.

For about five years, I've been conducting workshops in a wide variety of places, focused on "Team Ministries" or "Multiple Staff Ministries." Church workers trying to work effectively and happily in teams pay a great deal of attention to their formal roles in the organization. They have formal contracts with the pastor, the bishop, the conference, the presbytery, the local congregation, or some person or group of that sort. They spend long hours of discussion with each other in their team working out their informal assignments, developing informal contracts with each other, and seeking smooth and gratifying working relationships. What they have a very hard time doing is recognizing their tacit contracts with one another. Even when a tacit contract or tacit role is uncovered, the people who take part in it often deny that it exists. But an outside observer or consultant can often see the denied role quite plainly.

Suppose a consultant discovers that Mr. Brown is a **fight-stopper**. If the consultant can either remove Mr. Brown from a meeting or persuade him not to intervene in arguments or can even shush Mr. Brown whenever he tries to stop an argument, his function will suddenly be boldly (and perhaps painfully) revealed both to Mr. Brown and to his co-workers. Since, as Dr. George Bach has pointed out in **The Intimate Enemy**, we need to be able to fight if we are to develop intimacy with one another, the team may discover that Mr. Brown has been keeping the peace at the cost of allowing any meaningful relationships in the team to develop.

I don't want to suggest that systems try to do away with tacit roles. In the first place, that's not possible. In the second place, many tacit roles are good, and the system would be worse off without them. The problem with tacit roles in church staffs (or anywhere else) is that they're never examined; nobody has ever looked at them long enough or carefully enough to know whether the church or the team would be better off or worse off without them. Few of us ever wonder why our particular team needs a Fight-stopper or a Joke-board-keeper or a Doubting Thomas, and becomes uneasy when that tacit role is unfilled.

Let me suggest that the next time you get together for a staff retreat or a team-maintenance meeting (you **do** have those, don't you?), you spend a portion of your time seeing what tacit roles you can identify in your group. If you have some trouble identifying them, invite in an outsider whose job it will be to look for the tacit roles being taken in your system. When you know what is happening, you will be better able to plan, better able to meet the individual needs of team members, better able to maintain the strength and morale of the team, and more effective in performing the team tasks.

It hasn't been the same since Gloria left.

This article first appeared in PACE in 1973. The author, DR. KENNETH R. MITCHELL, was director of the Division of Religion and Psychiatry for The Menninger Foundation.

16
Religious Indifferentism and Professional Identity

Carl Lofy

I

Last week a pastor stopped in for a visit, to discuss ways he might "plug in" to our experimental program. I told him we were eager to have someone assist students to face their religious problems. Often these lie at the heart of other conflicts, especially with their parents. For example, it is not uncommon for them, while discussing things with their parents, to get "wiped out" or "put in their place" by a quotation from the Bible for which they have no response. Since courses in biblical theology are not readily available, they are often forced into silence and its resultant tension.

The pastor agreed that "someone" (he did not say who) should look into this, but added that he, for his part, wished "to do some group work—along the lines of sensitivity training." When asked what training he had for this, he said he had just completed a two week session himself. I explained that our Counseling Center provided these experiences through persons specifically trained in that area, and that what we really needed was someone to deal with the students' religious problems. "I wouldn't," he said, "feel very comfortable doing that."

His response was not untypical. There is increasing evidence that religious educators are tending to shy away from religious and doctrinal problems, in order to concentrate on issues less theological in nature, such as method, personality, social action, sensitivity, and the like. They feel less qualified in the areas for which they have been trained than they do in other areas about which they know little. Some educators tend to call everything religion or anything theology, and they cross disciplinary and even professional boundaries with abandon.

In an implicit, anonymous way every human act is, of course, religious in nature. But theology is not psychology, and religious training, though it should be sensitively done, is not sensitivity training. Theology as a science (or wisdom) is a discipline in its own right, with its own history, methods, and traditions. Some are finding the restraints of that discipline too confining.

Several things have resulted. The first is a sort of doctrinal in-difference. Doctrines such as the Trinity, Incarnation, Virgin-Birth, and Original Sin are often ignored or left unprobed. The Immaculate Conception, Assumption, and Ascension are seldom mentioned. Redemption is explained in solely psychological terms. Instead, religious educators are stressing "experience," "community," "human dynamics," "interpersonal relationships." Personal authenticity has become the central doctrine of our times. Sensitivity or emotional honesty are considered the legitimate marks of religiosity.

Much of this comes as a reaction to a dogmatism in which many of us were brought up. We were told it was important **what** we believed, rather than **how** we understood our beliefs and how we felt about them. A question dogmatists seldom ask is how you (or they!) feel about a certain doctrine. Their arguments stem mostly from tradition and authority. Aquinas once described these students as leaving their lectures convinced **that** this or that is so, but "with their minds empty as to **how** they are so."

There are deep-seated differences between this form of dog-matism and the thinking of many religious educators today. These differences are both epistemological and psychological in nature. They concern the nature of truth and the psychological uses one makes of truth or knowledge. For example, the old dogmatism tended to see truth as a body of knowledge. The "deposit of faith" was seen only (which it is also) as a series of dogmas to be passed on from one generation to another, from the death of the last apostle until the end of time. The need for each generation to re-examine dogma, to make it genuinely relevant and meaningful, was not emphasized. Doctrine became an answer book and remained basically Tridentine in its language and intent.

Today theologians stress that truth is a **personal characteristic**. A person is either "in truth" or not. Christ's answer to Pilate's question as to what is truth is valid for his followers today: "I am Truth." The Christian life, seen in this context, is a progressive process of verification, in its root meaning (**verum**) of "truth-ification." To be in truth (or light) is more important than to have truth.

Theologians today are emphasizing, as did Paul, that one can know all things, or "have all truth," and still be lost. They point out that, psychologically, one can use knowledge (or truth, in the abstract sense) to distance oneself from people, to control them or maintain superiority over them. Some teachers are the best examples of this, using their knowledge and lectures to keep students at bay. Administrators, including the hierarchy, often do the same. So do those who see themselves as "saved," others as "damned."

As a reaction to this situation many of today's religious educators feel a need to get close to people. Some consider doctrine a burden or even a curse, separating them from "the least of Christ's brethren." They wish to experience people as they are and as they (the educators) are—without special benefit of saving doctrine or presumed salvation. Under the reign of dogmatism they experienced a great dearth of emotional contact, precisely since feelings were never consulted. Today's educators wish to feel, to express, to be and to become, to grow and develop: all of which leads them to other areas, such as psychology, sensitivity training, social action and the like.

This is not all bad. In fact it's healthy. The problem comes when one is no longer fish or fowl. In the excitement of sensitivity, religious "happenings," close personal ties, and the like, doctrine sometimes gets slighted. I know one educator whose entire course on the Sacraments is, as he described it, "a series of human experiences." Obviously children should be helped to experience the sacraments as totally as possible. But no theology, or religion, can survive if all of its statements are drained of theological content.

On the heels of this increasing indifference toward doctrine comes **doctrinal indifferentism**—subtle and often unstated. It arises out of the belief that doctrine is irrelevant or out-dated and **is itself a doctrine**. If pushed far enough (that is, to the point of saying that, not only the **way** dogma has been presented but dogma-in-itself is irrelevant), this "doctrine" would be heretical. The problem is that, by definition, its proponents are indifferent even in regard to their "heretical status." Hence they tend to stay around, often unnoticed. Modern heresies are for the most part unexpressed. The most common one is that heresy makes no difference. In effect this means doctrine makes no difference.

This situation causes great suffering, especially to those who are victims of it. I recall the relief a friend experienced when she had to give up teaching because of pregnancy. She could finally admit, she told us, "how agnostic I feel."

In her case, as in others, indifferentism can be forced on educators. They are trained in theology and often would like to explore certain newer interpretations. But they are hired by a system that frequently fails to tolerate innovation or creative exploration. Many of those who pay their salaries still believe in the importance of passing on dogmas "intact." No one experiences less the right of academic freedom than these religious educators. Hence, rather than state their own uncertainties openly, they feel compelled to "play the game" as long as they can. Their heart is in one place, their role, title, and even language in another. This fact was brought home to me last month when a religious educator of some note said that she sees her audiences as "dead." She gives them "Jesus-talk," she said, "because I feel I have to. But I try to slip in as much on human dynamics as possible."

Her conflict and that of the pastor described earlier represent profound professional identity crises. The person feels neither here nor there: untrained to do what he or she feels important, unqualified or unable to confront his or her own field. The solution many people find for this temporary "professional schizophrenia" is to play the game for as long as possible and then to leave. Worse, some deceive themselves completely into thinking of themselves as (untrained) experts in some other field, or into thinking these other things are religious education. It takes a while, but only a short while, for their students to see through this. The educators soon become suspect, since they are manifestly ineffective in **two** fields. Thus, in some cases they end up lonely human beings, in need of great love. It is not uncommon for persons in such emotional deprivation to wind up in moral (as well as doctrinal) indifference. Ethics become as unimportant to them as dogma. Professional immaturity ends in personal irresponsibility. Their deception (and emptiness) is apparent least of all to themselves.

II

There is no easy way out of this dilemma. It is correct that genuine reform lays the axe to the root of the tree, namely, to the heart. We are to worship the Father in Spirit as well as in Truth. It **is** more important, in the last analysis, how one is than what one believes. But the contrary is also true: Spirit **and** truth. Doctrine is important. History, tradition, and content still belong in theology and religion, not for their own sake, but to help interpret life in the very act of their being interpreted **by** life.

It is impossible, and would be unwise, to return to the former dogmatism. Moreover, the great theologians of both the past and present have been profoundly steeped in philosophies and ideas not specifically theological. Augustine built on Plato and Plotinus; Aquinas on Aristotle. Rahner has been deeply influenced by Heidegger and Kant. But all of them are theologians! Philosphy, psychology, sensitivity experiences, sociology, political science—all, when properly grasped, feed new insights into theology. But too many religious educators are only going part way with them. Too many, for example, are **neither** theologian **nor** psychologist. Some try the other fields, then give them up as the going gets tough. They are neither-nor, avoiding the hard work of each field. To break the dilemma more will have to become **both-and**. They will have to become proficient in several areas. Or they will have to work closely with persons genuinely qualified in other areas. Otherwise they will be guilty of non-professionalism in their own field, and quackery in the other.

III

How important, then, is doctrine?

Very!

For the religious educator it has to remain the core of what he or she communicates. How and what one is as a person is more important than what one teaches. But one cannot long survive **in truth** when one's statements cease altogether being theological. To be in truth includes being what one professes, saying openly what one believes, expressing oneself professionally when one is being paid for that. As in all other things truth is found in synthesis, not polarity. Theologians must re-vist life. As persons they can grow and become. But as professionals they must also visit tradition and make the halls of doctrine come alive again—with new language, new metaphors, and new understanding—using these as searchlights to illumine the dark corridors of the as yet unknown and unexplored. As theologians they can shed light on many areas of genuine human concern. They can provide solutions to pressing and complex religious difficulties or at least share the burden of their complexity. Their theology should provide them strength to bear its own uncertainties, as well as the ambiguities of life itself. These very ambiguities will, in turn, refine and chasten their theology.

Augustine once said we should not be afraid of the thought of those he called "pagans." Rather, he said, theologians should make this thought their own, not by becoming pagans, but by becoming more insightful theologians.

The same can be said in our time of the so-called secular disciplines. Superficial dabbling is not enough. Penetration, insight, depth—all the fruits of hard scholarship—will restore to theology and religious education a new sort of fiber and heat that will deserve respectability and a hearing. What is needed is a commitment to **both** sides of the paradox: genuine secular learning with profound theological understanding.

This article first appeared in PACE in 1970. The author, CARL LOFY, did doctoral work in theology and psychology at Innsbruck, Austria, and is now professor of counseling at Mankato State University.

17

The DRE—A Parish Executive

John Bosio

During the past few years, a new phenomenon has appeared in the American parish—the Director of Religious Education. Today, more and more churches are hiring DREs because of the felt need of providing adequate opportunities for religious education to all members of the parish: adults, youth, and children. While a great deal has been said and written about the role of the DRE in the parish and about his or her qualities and competencies, I believe that DREs, whether they realize this or not, hold an executive position in the parish they serve. In this article, then, I should like to discuss the implications of this role.

In the business world, an executive is generally perceived as a person hired to implement specific policies or programs of action decided upon by the board of directors of a company or business. As such, the executive does not make policies, even though he or she may act as a consultant in the process of making policies and setting goals. Executives must be leaders: they must know how to communicate with people both above them and below them and be able to manage efficiently the resources available to them. Executives are accountable to those who have hired them for the effectiveness with which they act in their areas of responsibility.

In the same way, the DRE as a parish executive is a professional, hired to implement specific policies or programs of action decided upon by the religious education board and approved by the parish council and the pastor. DREs, therefore, are not hired to make policies about religious education for the parish they serve, even though they may act as resource persons and make recommendations in the process of making policies and setting goals. DREs are hired to execute and guide the parish in the implementation of its religious education policies. DREs are accountable to the parish through the religious education board and the parish council for the effectiveness with which they carry out the tasks for which they have been hired.

A key word in the process of understanding the qualities of the DRE as a parish executive is **effectiveness**.

I once saw in the office of a top executive a plaque with a quote from Peter Drucker which said: "Most executives are intelligent, imaginative, and knowledgeable. But that doesn't mean they're effective. And that's what it's all about. That's their job—to be effective, to get the right thing done!"

DREs as parish executives must be effective. DREs who are effective will move the parish forward because they will carry out efficiently the tasks they undertake. DREs who lack efficiency in their work will go around in circles. Little will get done, and parishes will not profit from their services.

What qualities can we look for in a DRE who is an effective parish executive? Directors of Religious Education who are effective parish executives are persons who (1) perceive themselves realistically, (2) know their place in the parish organizational structure, (3) understand clearly the tasks for which they have been hired, (4) are aware of the resources available to them, and (5) manage these resources efficiently.

1) EFFECTIVE DIRECTORS OF RELIGIOUS EDUCATION PERCEIVE THEMSELVES REALISTICALLY.

They know their assets and liabilities, their strong points and their weaknesses. They utilize their assets as fully as possible and work on their weaknesses. Effective DREs have confidence in themselves and their qualities; they know that they have something to contribute to the parish they serve. They are not threatened by the qualities and competencies of others, but rather welcome them. They know how to delegate responsibility especially in those areas where their abilities are slight. In short, DREs who are effective in their work are persons who have reached a certain level of personal maturity.

2) EFFECTIVE DREs KNOW THEIR PLACE IN THE PARISH ORGANIZATIONAL STRUCTURE.

They know where they fit in with the religious education board, the parish council, the other staff members, the parish school personnel, etc. This knowledge is essential. DREs, like any other executives, cannot function effectively without knowing to whom they are accountable, how much freedom they have to operate within the guidelines given them, how much authority they have over volunteer teachers and hired help, what role they are expected to play in the meetings of the religious education board, and whether or not they are to be members of the parish council.

3) EFFECTIVE DREs UNDERSTAND CLEARLY THE TASKS FOR WHICH THEY HAVE BEEN HIRED AND THE EXTENT OF THEIR RESPONSIBILITIES.

DREs' tasks and responsibilities are related to specific results which the parish wants to see achieved by hiring a professional. It may be the organization of a religious education program for children, for youth, for adults, a family centered program, or whatever other goals a parish may have. These goals are usually spelled out in the DRE's job description or contract.

Effective DREs give serious consideration to these goals or expected results before accepting the job, since once they sign the contract they will be held accountable for the effective implementation of the parish goals.

Effective DREs know not only the extent of their responsibilities, but also how to set for themselves an order of priorities among the tasks assigned to them by the parish. Then they can allocate sufficient personal efforts and parish resources for the successful achievement of each individual objective.

4) EFFECTIVE DREs ARE AWARE OF THE RESOURCES AVAILABLE TO THEM.

To begin with, they will make an inventory of all the resources given them by the parish. They will then attempt to match up the potential of these resources with the tasks they are expected to perform and the goals to be achieved. They must then determine whether or not the available resources are sufficient.

5) EFFECTIVE DREs AS PARISH EXECUTIVES MUST KNOW HOW TO MANAGE THE AVAILABLE RESOURCES EFFICIENTLY.

The efficient management of resources involves: the proper allocation of resources to each individual project according to priorities and needs; the proper use of the resources allocated; the accountability for the resources used; the ability on the part of the executive to evaluate present use of resources and to forecast future needs.

To summarize, DREs are parish executives. Effective DREs are persons who perceive themselves realistically, know their place in the parish organizational structure, understand clearly the tasks for which they have been hired, are aware of the resources available, and manage these resources efficiently.

To paraphrase Peter Drucker's statement quoted earlier: Most DREs are intelligent, imaginative, and knowledgeable. But that doesn't mean they are effective, and effectiveness is a quality they need. DREs, while developing all their competencies, must not neglect their executive qualities and potential. Without a certain degree of executive effectiveness DREs will fail to fulfill the expectations of those who hire them.

This article first appeared in PACE in 1976. The author, JOHN BOSIO, is Family Life Coordinator for the Archdiocese of Kansas City. This is one in a series of articles found in their entirety in PACE 7.

18
Memo to: Parish Professionals re: Coordinator as Administrator

Joseph C. Neiman

In a number of dioceses and parishes the coordinator is viewed as an administrator. Such a view is frowned upon among the parish professionals in their discussions about role. Religious especially wince at the term, finding it incompatible with their vocation. Perhaps it is more the meaning which we give to the term **administration**, rather than the actual concept itself, since fundamentally the word **administration** is related to ministry.

The word "administer" comes from two Latin words: the preposition, **ad**, and the verb, **ministro**. The verb means "to serve" and the preposition when referring to persons takes the meaning of "among." Thus, the word means "to serve among." Such a definition immediately calls to mind the whole New Testament tradition expressed so well by Paul: "Let love make you serve one another" (Gal. 5:13).

Our culture, over the years, began to equate the word **administration** with **bureaucracy**, which comes from the French word for "desk" and the Greek word for "rule" (**kratia**). We conjure up images of a person sitting behind a desk carrying out numerous policies and programs in a most effective way. Or we see such a person attending numerous meetings, handling budgets and books, carrying on routine correspondence, and in general running the "system." Indeed such a lifestyle does exist among parish professionals whether they call themselves administrators or resource persons. Such persons also function according to the time concept of **chronos**, that is, according to a fixed schedule of hours and days.

On the other hand, the more ancient concept of ministry inherent in the word itself is somewhat closer to the idyllic "role" described so frequently by parish professionals: "a bridge builder; a person of faith, of commitment, of hope, of prayer; a person who listens, consults, and discerns; a visionary, innovator, prophet; a person who creates within a team; and so forth."

Ministry requires **faith** to be sure, but the faith which is demanded is not mere human feeling or adherence to the law. "We know that a man is put right with God only through faith in Jesus Christ, never by doing what the Law requires" (Gal. 2:16). And yet we make a law out of our own creations like group process.

Secondly, ministry involves a **lifestyle which is of Christ.** While we cannot set a rigid pattern for each person to follow, nevertheless Christian ministry demands that we "put on compassion, kindness, humility, gentleness, and patience. Be helpful to one another, forgive one another whenever any of you has a complaint against someone else. . . . And to all these add love which binds all things together in perfect unity" (Col. 3:13ff). Frequently at meetings we complain to one another about the pastor, the others in our team, or certain ignorant members of the parish who bug us.

Thirdly, service among the community (administration) involves **teaching the Word of God**. "Teach and instruct each other with all wisdom. . . . Everything you do or say, then, should be done in the name of the Lord Jesus . . ." (Col. 3:17). It is an awesome responsibility to decide which of the many things that strike our fancy (films, current events, books, examples, etc.) are actually "of God."

Lastly, administration (ministry) involves hard work and suffering, as Paul's testimony reminds us (Col. 1 and 2); and humble service as Christ's example shows us (John 13). It also necessitates that we follow the concept of time termed **kairos**, or the **Day of the Lord** (1 Thess. 5). When we measure with **chronos** we can easily mistake activity for accomplishment or look for success in numbers; when we follow **kairos**, success will come "like a thief in the night" (1 Thess. 5:2).

Administration, therefore, is not really a dirty word but a word for ministry which requires sweaty service. But it also has its rewards. Paul writes to Timothy that "the elders who do good work as leaders should be considered worthy of receiving double pay, especially for those who work hard at preaching and teaching" (1 Tim. 5:17).

This article first appeared in PACE in 1972. The author, JOSEPH C. NEIMAN, has been coordinator of research and development at Divine Word International Centre, author of **Coordinators** (Saint Mary's Press), and a member of a task-force for upgrading the profession of religious education coordinator.

19
The Religious Educator as Spiritual Director

Maria Harris

In his address to the Nobel Foundation in Stockholm upon receipt of the 1976 Nobel Prize for Literature, Saul Bellow spoke of a struggle "at the center," out of which has come "an immense, painful longing for a broader, more flexible, fuller, more coherent, more comprehensive account of what we human beings are, who we are, and what this life is for." The contemporary longing of which Bellow spoke is not new to DREs and parish coordinators; as ministers to the people of local parishes, and confidantes of many, we know the longing firsthand. Many of us experience it ourselves.

I think it accurate to say that the longing has led to a new demand made on the already far too busy DRE. To the request that we be Scripture scholars, counselors, theologians, catechists, and janitors, there is the growing request that we take on the role and function of the spiritual director. This article is a beginning exploration, a tentative probe in the direction of understanding what such a request might mean, with the hope that many others will join in such exploration.

I want to reflect on three issues: the meaning of spirituality; the grounding and point of departure for the religious educator's spirituality; and the nature of the "direction" that a religious educator might give. I want to emphasize that I write as a religious educator, scouting somewhat unfamiliar territory, and that my comments are offered as a rough map and not a landscape. In addition, I approach the task with reservation akin to that recorded in the Hasidic tale: "When Rabbi Mendel was in Kotzk, the rabbi of that town asked him, 'Where did you learn the art of silence?' He was on the verge of answering the question, but then changed his mind and practiced his art." Although it is essential that one practice the art of spirituality, it is also necessary to take the risk of speaking.

THE MEANING OF SPIRITUALITY

In all cultures, that which is traditionally believed to be the vital principle or animating force within living beings has been given the name "spirit." Because it also means to **breathe** and to be **alive**, for us humans spirit begins in bodiliness and is rooted in the earth. The other meaning of Spirit, however, has been as the name of the One who is the Presence-With-Us. In the relationship of this Spirit of God to the spirits of us humans, spirituality begins.

In the Christian religious tradition, the noun **spiritualitas**, meaning the formal and creative core of religious existence, is found as early as the fifth and sixth centuries, and is quite common in the twelfth and thirteenth centuries. In the seventeenth century the French **spiritualité** was established in its technical sense to indicate the personal relationship of human beings and God. As the subjective side of the relationship was more and more stressed, the richness of mutuality, relationship, and what Buber calls **dialogue** became lost, and in time spirituality came to have a superficial, trivialized, and even banal meaning for many.

Now, however, we are aware of having run dry, and we have begun to return to the sources. One such source is the sequence for Pentecost, the centuries-old hymn **Veni Sancte Spiritus**. Its rich Latin cadences are reminders that the human word to the divine is the simple yet desperately urgent one, "Come."

> **Veni, Sancte Spiritus,**
> **Et emitte caelitus**
> **Lucis tuae radium.**
>
> **Veni, Pater Pauperum,**
> **Veni, Dator Munerum**
> **Veni, Lumen Cordium**
>
> **Consolator optime,**
> **Dulcis hospes animae,**
> **Dulce refrigerium.**
>
> **In labore requies,**
> **In aestu temperies,**
> **In fletu solatium.**
>
> **O Lux beatissima**
> **Reple cordis intima**
> **Tuorum fidelium.**
>
> **Sine tuo numine**
> **Nihil est in homine**
> **Nihil est innoxium.**

I would suggest that for the religious educator, the meaning of Christian spirituality can be understood in rediscovering the life which this monumental and ancient prayer of the church symbolizes. **Sine tuo numine**: literally, "Without your Godhead, your numinous presence, there is nothing in human beings, nothing that is innocent." Spirituality begins as the activity by which we acknowledge that we are without possibility in the presence of all Possibility; without affectivity in the presence of Love; without vision in the presence of ineffable Light. "Come, Father-Mother of the poor; Come Giver of gifts; Come, Light of hearts." The painful longing of which Bellow writes, the passion for fullness, coherence, and comprehensiveness finds voice: "Best of Comforters, Sweet Guest of the soul, Sweet refreshment."

**Rest in labor
Cool respite in heat
Comfort in weeping.**

**O most blessed Light
Fill the inmost hearts
Of your faithful.**

The meaning of spirituality, however, also bears within it a second element. Although it is the expression of the humans asking for the Spirit of God, the asking is that the Spirit come to us not as Soul to souls, but as Comforter to beings who experience the full range of bodiliness and of flesh. Spirituality is the touching and being touched of human, incarnate persons: **Lava quod est sordidum. Riga quod est aridum, Sana quod est saucium.** This is the prayer of the human who knows what it is to be parched and dry: "Wash the stained one; water the parched; heal the wounded." **Flecte quod est rigidum, fove quod est frigidum, rege quod est devium:** "Make supple the rigid. Warm the cold. Straighten the crooked."

This second quality of spirituality is the one more pressing today—our need for the presence of God in the midst of our humanness; our conviction that, as with each other, so too we and the earth are sisters and brothers; our sense that if a true spirituality is to animate us, it must be sacramental. By "sacramental" here I mean the affirmation that physical, material, and bodily reality has a spiritual dimension, and that God is revealed through bread and wine and earth and land and human being. A spirituality without this sense has still not come to grips with a Word made flesh. It is still in danger of being irreverent toward non-human nature: water, grass, trees, animals. More critically, if it lacks the understanding that bodies need shelter and healing and refreshment (warm the cold, straighten the crooked, water the parched), it is in danger of becoming narcissistic and individualistic. A spirituality with this dimension, however, has its own inner rhythm. Set in a corporate context, where all human beings are united with one another and with the earth, it can be the source by which we are inwardly animated, turn outward to others and to the divine, and return to rest in our own centers, at the same time linked to that Center which is the still point of our turning world.

POINT OF DEPARTURE

The proliferation of programs in spirituality and pastoral ministry is double-edged. On the one hand, if religious educators are seeking to enhance their abilities **as** religious educators by participating in these programs, all well and good. But if we are choosing them because we feel that the religious education profession is becoming dry, we may lose the opportunity for ministry and education discovered in the last fifteen years precisely because we have taken a stance as a group of **educators** and have been slowly but surely growing as a profession. At some point it becomes necessary to hone one's own self-definition and, if for years we have been religious educators, something troubling may underlie the switching of self-definition to spiritual director. What I would suggest instead is that our point of departure for investigating spirituality with others is precisely our role and stance as religious educators. The communal nature of religious education, especially as it occurs in parishes, is an ideal setting to pursue the issues spirituality raises, but always **from the rootedness that comes from being a religious educator.** Two tasks appear to me to be particularly important at this time: the critical examination of forms of spirituality and the critical examination of the language and images of prayer.

In Whitehead's well-known formulation, a religious education is one that inculcates duty and reverence. With reference to duty, Whitehead points out that it arises from our potential control over the course of events. "Where attainable knowledge could have changed the issue, ignorance has the guilt of vice." It is the peculiar responsibility of the educator to ask "Why?" "How do we know?" "Why is this so?" "On what grounds?" Now, if forms of spirituality which are fresh, humane, and appropriate to our own times are to come alive, grow, and be a source of religious integrity, they need the educator's asking of critical questions. The twin dangers of forms of unthinking emotionalism on the one hand or theological abstruseness on the other must be examined (especially as these appear in liturgy and preaching). The ever present danger of manipulation of people's feelings, especially at the hands—or voice—of a present day Elmer Gantry or Sister Sara must be avoided. The rush to judgment about relative degrees of holiness or moral goodness, already familiar to us through over-reliance on stage theory, must be questioned. Examination, questioning, and critical judgment are the educator's tasks, and for the sake of the church as a whole and of the genuine spirituality that is growing, we cannot accept what simply feels good, or what works. Groups of teachers need to suggest criteria and raise tough issues in the form of such questions as: what do we choose to look at and what do we label "religious"? What basic understandings seem to underlie these forms: about God? about human beings? What seem to be the purposes of these forms? Where did we learn to express our prayer life this way? Why?

The second contribution of religious educators lies in the examination of the images, symbols, and language of prayer. Can we hear the person, man or woman, who is truly ill at ease addressing God as Trinity; as Father; as Son; as Lord; as Master? Do we realize that all our language is metaphor, and that even the image of Father is an attempt to say that the one who created the world and nurtured the galaxies is God-with-us as the One who Cares? The issue here is not only the sexism of most of our language about God but the deeper one of the images, symbols, and metaphors we have for God forming the basis of our divine-human relationship. The response is not the often made yet somehow flippant suggestion that the divine be called "She" or even "He-She," but the far more difficult and profound search for appropriate images for the One beyond all images who remains the Beyond in our midst. Those who educate others religiously, which is to say those who examine how humans are bound to ultimate origin, deepest meaning, and final destiny, are, in my judgment, responsible to engage in this enormous task.

DIRECTION AND SPIRITUAL DIRECTION

William Barry, the former head of the Institute for Contemporary Spirituality at Weston College in Cambridge, Massachusetts, speaks of spiritual direction as that form of pastoral ministry whose specific purpose is to help persons relate to the living God, to help them let God relate to them, and to let their lives be determined and judged by that relationship. For the DRE, this help will probably not be given in the one-to-one situation of director and directee, although this possibility need not necessarily be excluded. It is more likely, however, that the form of the direction already exists in the round of classes, courses, programs, teachers' meetings, and visits that form the core of the DREs' daily activity. The spiritual direction given arises from the religious education present **now** in the parish and from the underlying philosophy upon which the pursuit of the religious rests, wherever the DRE works. If the religious education program which the parish **is** is child-centered, the spirituality of the parish may also be so, although unconsciously. But if the parish has a self-consciousness as a community of people engaged in a journey, then the spirituality of journey will be the one that is reflected. It is this understanding which can, in my judgment, support the spirituality of all.

A religious people lives in the context of journey. The journey spoken of here takes a lifetime; God is where the people are going. The journey has stages, pitfalls, risks. Like all journeys, it involves meeting wise old men and wise old women—and every parish educator would do well to insure that the generations meet as the journey goes on. A journey also involves periods of darkness, where there is much doubt, but again, if the people are journeying together, the faith of the community can support the doubting one during such times. Finally, the journey involves two great challenges. The first is the challenge to **hold on**: to grasp with fingertips if necessary, till the arms ache and the back bends and the sweat runs down the face. The second challenge is to **let go**: to say yes as Hammarskjöld did, knowing not when, or how, or to whom, or why, but only that at some point, one has been addressed by Being, and the only appropriate answer is "Yes."

And what is the journey toward? What is its **direction**? All of the evidence is, of course, not in, but thus far, the Christian religious tradition has affirmed these: the journey is in the direction of **adulthood**; the maturity of the sons and daughters of God is in the image of the Christ. The journey is in the direction of **wholeness**, not so much in the psychological as in the sacramental sense already mentioned, where one becomes at one with the Holy, with other persons, and with the universe. And the journey is in the direction of **death**, the final waning of one's powers, until coming to rest in the arms of the earth with whom one has gradually become a friend.

Those, however, are the penultimate directions. The final direction, toward which all of the Christian tradition points, and to which the religious educator in this setting gives testimony, is the direction of **resurrection**. The hope of that resurrection is sung at the completion of the **Veni Sancte Spiritus:**

> **Da virtutis meritum.**
> **Da salutis exitum.**
> **Da perenne gaudium.**

Give reward to goodness. Give salvation at the end. Give joy everlasting. Amen. Alleluia.

In the naming of directions such as these, today's religious educators might make significant contributions to the contemporary church and to the world in which that church exists. Perhaps the Spirit will grant that it be so.

FOR FURTHER READING

Barry, William. "The Contemplative Attitude Fostered by Spiritual Direction: Its Possibilities for Campus Ministry," in **NICM Journal**, Spring 1977, pp. 109-117.

de Castillejo, Irene. **Knowing Woman**. New York: Harper Colophon, 1973.

Maloney, George. **Inward Stillness**. Denville, NJ: Dimension, 1976.

Merton, Thomas. **Contemplative Prayer**. New York: Herder and Herder, 1969.

Rahner, Karl (ed.). **Sacramentum Mundi**. Volume 6. New York: Herder and Herder, 1970. See especially Josef Sudbrack, "Spirituality," pp. 147-157.

Whitehead, Alfred North. **The Aims of Education**. New York: Macmillan, 1929.

This article first appeared in PACE in 1977. The author, MARIA HARRIS, is at present associate professor of religion and education at Andover Newton Theological School. Her most recent work is **Portrait of Ministry**.

PART TWO

Reports from the Field

1
A Statement of DRE Tasks

Catherine F. Siffin

The following statement was formulated by APARE—the Association of Parish Administrators of Religious Education (of the Archdiocese of Indianapolis)—established in April 1977. APARE's purposes are to foster the spiritual and professional growth of its membership through a support and service organization and to clarify and strengthen the role of DREs in the Archdiocese. To further these aims, the program committee chose "A Self-definition of the DRE" as the topic for its first working meeting in October of '77. The interest generated was so great that an ad hoc committee was appointed to synthesize the tentative conclusions of the October meeting into major categories. Two more membership meetings were held in January and February of '78 to review and refine the work of the ad hoc committee, with mailings of the evolving statement to all absent members. Finally, the total membership of APARE at its annual spring meeting with the Archdiocesan Office of Catholic Education adopted the statement as it is reproduced below.

The two questions which the membership considered in formulating this statement were: As DREs, what are we doing now? As DREs, what do we think we should be doing? As they considered these questions, they realized that priority is often given to the tasks of a DRE directly pertaining to the here and now—the practical jobs of producing programs, managing personnel, etc. (tasks V and VI below)—whereas little explicit consideration is given to the important tasks which must precede and accompany these "practical" ones if they are to be carried out effectively. In studying the statement, then, we ask you to take special note of the **order** in which the tasks are listed.

The purpose of this statement is to provide a challenge to and guidelines for DREs, and also to provide a concrete, understandable description of the role of the DRE which will help promote understanding of that role among the groups served by DREs: pastors and parish teams, parishioners, parish councils, boards of education, and perhaps persons interested in entering the DRE profession. One aspect of this purpose is to indicate "limits" to the DRE role, because we realize that a great deal of misunderstanding exists about how much a DRE could and should be expected to accomplish. At the same time, we hope to develop some understanding of the real

responsibility of the total parish community for religious education
—i.e., the DRE may direct and coordinate this responsibility, but
certainly many others and, ultimately, the whole community, are
involved.

We have therefore attempted to draw widespread attention to
the statement. For example, a series of articles on the DRE tasks is
running in our archdiocesan newspaper, **The Criterion**; in each article
a DRE describes his/her experiences in carrying out one of the tasks.
Also one committee person has been appointed to contact the Priests'
Senate and the Principals' Association to explain the statement and
invite comments about it. Now we hope that the publication of the
statement in **PACE** will attract the interest of other professional associations of DREs and of individuals. We would welcome your comments and suggestions. (Address: Don Kurre, Secretary of APARE,
6950 East 46th Street, Indianapolis, Indiana 46226.)

A STATEMENT OF DRE TASKS

I. Continuing Spiritual and Professional Development of the DRE

The DRE takes responsibility for personal and spiritual growth
and prayer, as well as for a professional growth process that
includes peer association (through APARE or other informal
gatherings), meetings, seminars, and reading.

The DRE takes responsibility for the prudent utilization of
funds budgeted for such growth.

II. Planning for Parish Religious Education

Planning is a major responsibility of the DRE. Planning is
future oriented and requires lead-time.

Effective Religious Education requires planning for:
1. assessing needs, defining goals and objectives, designing curriculum
2. recruitment and training of: catechists for children and
   youth, adult resource persons, and leaders of adult
   Religious Education
3. providing resources and
4. the budgeting of personal and parish time, resources,
   and finances

III. Participating as a Member of the Pastoral Team

The DRE is to share the responsibility of developing and sustaining a pastoral team marked by trust, dialogue, prayer, and celebration.

The specific input of the DRE to the team would be as resource person for insights pertinent to the religious educational growth of the parish and the team.

IV. Sharing Responsibility of the Board of Education

The DRE is to share the responsibility of developing and sustaining a Board of Education marked by:
1. awareness of Total Catholic Education
2. trust
3. dialogue
4. prayer and
5. celebration

The specific input of the DRE to the Board would be to
1. initiate and implement policy
2. inform and report
3. clarify job expectations
4. prepare a budget for Parish Religious Education
5. deepen awareness of total Catholic education
6. and possibly serve as Administrative Officer to the Board

V. Managing Office and Personnel for Religious Education

As administrator of Religious Education in the parish, the DRE is responsible for managing (an office) and communicating to the parish and community at large.

Office management includes:
1. definition of and delegation of tasks
2. supervision of staff (paid and volunteer)
3. record keeping and
4. budget control

VI. Creating, Implementing, and Coordinating for Religious Education

The DRE's present concerns are:
1. designing curriculum and learning opportunities to meet the real and expressed needs

2. recruiting, training, and supporting volunteers
3. acquiring and organizing resources
4. evaluating personnel, curriculum, and learning opportunities
5. serving as resource person to total Catholic education

This article first appeared in PACE in 1978. The author, CATHERINE F. SIFFIN, worked for five years as DRE for adults at St. Charles Parish in the Archdiocese of Indianapolis. She is now taking "time off" for study and writing.

2
What Coordinators Think about Their Profession

Richelle Pearl Koller

Last year the Association of Coordinators of Religious Education (a voluntary professional organization formed by coordinators to meet their needs) conducted a survey among the 180 coordinators employed in the Archdiocese of St. Paul and Minneapolis. The purpose of the survey was four-fold:

1) To assess the needs, interests, and concerns of coordinators in the Archdiocese.
2) To gather data for the Association's Executive Board that could be used to determine future programming and services offered to the membership.
3) To enable the Association on the basis of its findings to make recommendations to the Archdiocesan Education Center and other pertinent Archdiocesan groups working with the coordinators.
4) To build the Association's image among the coordinators as a professional organization that exists to meet their needs.

Each of the people surveyed received a copy of the attached questionnaire and was asked to reflect on the questions and answer them. Then each of the Association's executive board members was assigned to specific coordinators and asked to set up interviews with them in small groups. At these sessions, the groups discussed their responses to the questionnaire as well as to the other issues that arose. The results of these sessions were then reported back to the executive board and compiled. In dealing with the results of the survey, no attempt was made to be scientific or numerical in tallying responses. Rather the attempt was made to group the comments under concern areas, reporting only those items that were frequently and consistently mentioned and which seemed to reflect the thinking of the majority of the coordinators in the area.

Before examining specific results of the survey, a few general observations should be noted. The caliber of person working in this profession is most impressive—highly talented and creative. The coordinators displayed a deep sense of commitment to the church and a true desire to be of service to the Christian community. They are willing to work and work hard to pass on the faith which they have received.

In this work of passing on the faith, the coordinators cited the following background experiences as most helpful to them:

1) Theological training, particularly in-depth graduate study and course work.
2) Educational experiences—teaching itself, as well as a study of the learning process and theory of education.
3) Administrative experience—any practical experience either in a school or business that aided them to acquire knowledge and skills in the areas of organization, personnel, budgeting, management, scheduling, and public relations.
4) Experiences in leadership and working with groups.

Many coordinators indicated that they had no accurate concept of what the job of religious education director involved prior to becoming a coordinator. Most misconceptions centered around the tension involved in being an administrator versus being an educator. Coordinators said they had no realization of the amount of administrative detail in which they were to become involved and felt administrative skill was just assumed by those hiring. Thus, when dealing with background experiences that would have been helpful prior to entering the profession, the following were frequently cited:

1) Training in administration, organizational management, and budgeting.
2) Training in how to work with volunteers.

3) Some kind of internship comparable to practice teaching.
4) Particularly on the part of those who entered the profession from an elementary school background, an expressed desire for more theological training.
5) On the part of those who had theological degrees, particularly former seminarians, a need for teaching and administrative skills and methods of bringing their theological understandings into religious education programs.

While the coordinators felt that a lack of understanding about the nature of the profession was a weakness in their preparation, they also expressed concern regarding the image of the profession held by pastors, boards of education, parish councils, and priests.

Some ten to fifteen years ago, the profession of religious education coordinator originated, in part at least, in response to the closing of Catholic elementary schools. A coordinator was hired to run a CCD program for children, and so the term "coordinator" became synonymous in the minds of many with a "person who deals with the religious education of young children."

An equally significant reason for the rise of this profession was the growing parish awareness that the majority of their youth (elementary through senior high) were no longer in Catholic schools. Many parishes came to recognize that their education efforts and priorities were aimed at the minority of their young people and so took steps to readjust this imbalance.

With the growth in parish awareness of the needs of teenage youth in the public schools and with the decline in the number of priests, particularly the young assistants who had usually worked with the adolescents, the role of the coordinator expanded. Soon the term coordinator came to mean "a person who deals with all dimensions of religious education—pre-school through senior citizen." Many coordinators working in such a situation experience heavy frustration and feel overworked, and their morale is low since they feel little support. Despite these frustrations, they like their job because they feel that they are serving the Church and because of the creative possibilities they see emerging in the profession.

One of the creative possibilities they see is the movement toward team, or shared, ministry where the coordinator's job becomes more specialized and the coordinator is recognized as part of a pastoral team. Coordinators like this trend toward shared ministry and find it very satisfying to work as a member of a team.

However, the maturation and growth of the profession combined with the trend toward shared ministry has led coordinators to recognize the need for job clarification and role delineation. No longer is it easy to define what a coordinator is. More and more it is imperative that pastors and parish boards clarify what it is they are looking for when they hire "a coordinator." Do they want an elementary, secondary, or adult education coordinator; a youth worker; a liturgist; a parish worker; a pastoral counselor? All of these are distinct jobs, demanding different skills. Not all, however, are mutually exclusive. Clarification of role and job description would help to eliminate misunderstandings for both the parish and the person hired.

Coordinators see that this profession has opened, particularly to the laity, a new form of ministry in the Church and that it can be a great impetus toward developing a Church in which the lay members assume more and more responsibility in the Christian community. It is this potential that stimulates and encourages people to remain in the profession.

Yet coordinators still have a strong feeling that their job is not understood by the clergy and boards of education, and that they are not dealt with as professional people. The coordinators are not looking for or expecting a utopia, an ideal working situation devoid of problems, conflicts, and frustrations. But they do feel that they have a right to expect some things, such as adequate office space, professional secretarial help, and some kind of general salary scale, as norms. The concern expressed here is that, particularly where lay people are concerned, it is each person for himself or herself at the bargaining table, that the tendency on the part of a board and pastors is to hire the lowest salaried person rather than to hire on the basis of competence. If there were some diocesan salary guidelines based on qualifications and experience, it would assist the individual in negotiating a wage at the local level.

A deep concern exists among lay coordinators, particularly among the men, regarding job security. These are men who want to work in the church, who are trained to do so and who want to make this their life's profession, but who fear remaining in it because it lacks security as evidenced in:

1) How easily a parish will hire one or two nuns for the price of one lay person, frequently displacing the lay person who had no intentions of leaving the parish.
2) How difficult it is for a man to consider raising a family on some salaries offered him. Coordinators are not looking for an executive's salary; they would like to be offered some-

thing in the salary area more in keeping with their training and today's cost of living.

3) How quickly a person gets to the "top," so to speak, in this profession, so that when his or her salary reaches the top he or she soon becomes the most expendable person. When a parish budget is to be cut, this one salary alone will knock out a huge sum.

4) How frequently a woman will be hired over a man because it might be less expensive.

These insecurities from the professional standpoint are what many coordinators see as an explanation for why people leave this profession so quickly. At the same time they see this transitoriness as hurting the Church and the parish community since it does not allow any continuity to develop at the parish level.

With all due respect to the women's liberation movement, it seems imperative (particularly in light of the declining number of priests) that we keep this area of ministry open to lay men, not merely in word, but in reality. We need male as well as female leadership in the Church.

Another aspect of the job that coordinators find frustrating is the work load and time expectations placed on them by a parish. Coordinators recognize that this is not a job comparable to a forty hour work week, but then it is not an eighty hour week either. There needs to be some balance. While it is essential that the individual establish his or her own balance and priorities, a parish needs to re-examine the job and its expectations of the individual.

Perhaps a source of deeper frustration among coordinators is a feeling of lack of priority and support for their work as evidenced in parish priorities and budgeting which tend to be: parish school, CCD, other, adult education, in that order.

A final area of concern shared by coordinators is the lack of evaluative tools for the profession as a whole. Coordinators are doing all kinds of things, producing all kinds of programs, but how do you evaluate the total job, the total impact? Coordinators are looking not so much for tools to evaluate this or that specific activity as they are for some critical means to analyze the profession as a whole. Until recently we have been too young a profession to develop such evaluative criteria, but perhaps we have come now to the point where this kind of tool needs to be developed.

These, then, are some of the concerns shared by coordinators in this region. It is my suspicion that the data we uncovered in our survey is not unique to our archdiocese but is shared by others across the country. It is my hope that in the next few years we might join together to strengthen the profession and make it an even more viable form of ministry in the Church.

QUESTIONS FOR REFLECTION

(1) In looking over your job as coordinator what experiences in your background best prepared you for this work? (2) What kind of training or experiences do you wish you had had prior to assuming the job of a coordinator? (3) What are the two or three most pressing problems or concerns facing you as a coordinator? (4) What do you think are the strengths and weaknesses of the profession of religious education coordination? (5) If you had a magic wand and could do one thing to improve this profession what would you do? (6) What do you experience as the greatest need for in-service training in your work? (7) How do you think the Association can be of service to you in meeting your needs, concerns, etc.? (8) Do you spend your work time the way you would like to spend it, or are there areas you wish you could change, or eliminate? (9) From your vantage point why do you think that the average life span of a coordinator in a parish is about three years?

This article first appeared in PACE in 1974. Later, in 1976, it was presented as part of an address in Philadelphia at the National Convention of the Religious Education Association. The author, RICHELLE PEARL KOLLER, is former president of the Association of Coordinators of Religious Education in the Archdiocese of St. Paul and Minneapolis, and is director of religious education at Christ the King Parish.

3

Accountability: To Whom and for Whom?

William V. Coleman

Sister Mary of Holy Sincerity is a parish religious education coordinator. No one works harder at her job than Sister Mary. No one wants to be more honest and objective than she. Last week's diocesan conference on "Accountability in Religious Education" was a real challenge to her. She left the conference with the determination to be accountable.

When she returned to the convent she shared her high hopes with her friend, Sister Saint Thomas the Doubtful. Sister Thomas had a few problems. She wondered to whom Sister Mary meant to be accountable—to parents, to the pastor, to the diocesan authorities, to her teachers, to her students, to God? She also wondered who in this long list, excepting God, wanted her to be accountable and who would know what to do if she tried to be accountable.

Sister Thomas had other problems, too. She wondered what Sister Mary would be accountable for—knowledge of doctrine, growth in faith, loyalty to the church or the parish, the good manners of the children, the smooth administration of the program, or the orthodoxy of what was said in each and every classroom?

At the end of the evening, Sister Thomas identified one more problem, the terms of accountability. "How would Sister Mary measure any of the things she decided to be accountable for?", she mused. That night Sister Thomas went to a quiet rest, knowing she had cast all the doubts upon the subject of accountability. Sister Mary of Holy Sincerity, however, did not sleep at all. What had seemed like a perfectly reasonable thing to do, be accountable, gave her nightmares all night long.

Our imaginary story highlights four questions which haunt the sincere religious educator who seeks to be accountable. The four questions are:

1) To whom should I be accountable?
2) Is he or she ready to receive my accountability?
3) What should I be accountable for?
4) What words and measures shall I use to express my accountability?

WHO IS OUR LEADER?

Administrative confusion is rife in U.S. Catholic parishes. In some, the pastor is the sole decision-maker. In others, the clergy of the parish, the parish staff, the parish council, the school board, or some combination of these make the decisions. In addition, some decision-making power may be vested in diocesan offices, or in the school or CCD faculties, or in the parents of the children in the programs.

The first step for religious educators who want to be accountable is to decide to whom they will be accountable. Living in a parish for a year or two will, usually, yield that information. In some parishes the parish council meets regularly but only as a rubber stamp for the pastor. In other parishes the pastor does little more than execute the decisions of the parish council. In still others there is an intricate interrelationship of several parish bodies. Religious educators must watch the decision-making process in the parish and then attempt to bring all decision-makers together into one working whole for the purpose of accepting their accountability. This may require another **ad hoc** structure, but is necessary in order to avoid being caught in a crossfire of intergroup struggle for authority.

PREPARING THE GROUND

It is something of the measure of the vitality of religious education that it seeks to be accountable. In many fields accountability is demanded by a supervisor and only begrudgingly given by a field worker. In U.S. religious education, the shoe is on the other foot. It is the field workers, the religious educators, who are seeking to be accountable. In many cases, the supervisors are not yet ready to receive that accountability.

Religious educators can put themselves into the position of the anxious boy who wants to explain to his unconcerned parents why he was late for supper. Actually, the parents enjoyed the privacy brought by his being late and are not at all troubled by his tardiness. As he explains his actions, he triggers guilt feelings in them. This, in turn, urges them to pick at his story so they can feel they are good parents. In the end, little is achieved.

So, for example, one diocesan director spent two full months preparing an elaborate report of the work of his office for the bishop. The bishop knew little about religious education. The report embarrassed him. To protect his position, he tried to find small inconsistencies in the report and demand that they be corrected. The director was crestfallen, for the whole thrust of his report was unnoticed. Only a few minor inconsistencies were ever discussed.

Before persons can be accountable, then, their supervisors must be interested in the subject and able to respond to a report. Accountability presupposes enough knowledge in the supervisor to be able to discuss the report with the field worker. It also presupposes a desire to do this.

Thus the second task of the religious educator who wishes to be accountable is to confront the pastor or other parish leaders and find out whether accountability is wanted and, if it is wanted, whether the leaders are able to understand what will be presented. This may take time. Yet a year or two spent preparing the ground for accountability is a better investment than time spent preparing reports which will not or cannot be understood.

THE SUBJECT OF ACCOUNTABILITY

Religious education in the U.S. is a wide field. It includes both evangelization and catechesis, both the invitation to faith and the explication of the traditional explanations of the articles of faith. In some cases, it also assumes responsibility for loyalty to the parish and the wider institutional church, the good behavior of the students and even the smooth administration of programs.

Can any religious educator be accountable for all these aspects of his or her work? Obviously, the answer to this question is "No." But the religious educator can and should be responsible for initiating or maintaining programs which have an inner thrust toward realistic goals.

One parish religious education coordinator tried to be accountable for the faith of her subjects. When she did, she assumed responsibility for the free interaction of God and the students. Her accountability was presumptuous. She was also doomed to failure, for not all her students would respond in faith to the invitation of the Lord and the Lord will not always invite all students to follow him in the way the religious education coordinator expected. The Spirit of the Lord breathes where and how it wills.

On the other hand, another coordinator felt responsible only for programs which seemed to have the potential for growth and development. She based her judgment on the best of contemporary writing and scholarship. While she was never sure what was happening in the faith life of individuals, she was able to judge and evaluate her programs by the standards she had set for them.

Our second religious educator is realistic. Her focus is on workable programs. This is all she felt able to provide. It was all she was willing to be accountable for. She refused to be accountable for the faith growth of her students, for their behavior, for some imaginary canon of orthodoxy. Her critics say she is too easy on herself. She retorts that she is realistic. We would have to agree with her rather than with her critics. A coordinator cannot be responsible for those things over which she has no control.

THE TERMS OF ACCOUNTABILITY

People who come to religious education with a business background tend to concretize the terms of accountability. Like many social scientists they operationalize abstract concepts in easily measured behavior. Thus, faith is equated with attendance at Mass on Sunday. Charity is measured in money given to the poor. Social scientists, educators and business leaders are now beginning to see the ir-rationality of this approach. Journals of education and sociology are filled with the reaction to this kind of operationalism. Yet, it continues to be popular among rank and file educators who took their training a decade ago. Many religious educators are also in the camp with these teachers and administrators. They are seeking in vain for good operationalizations of religious concepts. It is the paradox of religious education, if not all education, that what is measurable is most peripheral to the core of the work. What is most central is least measurable. Prudent religious educators will be most careful on this point and not allow themselves to become trapped by the terms of their accountability. They will insist on keeping the field vague and insightful rather than concrete and empirical. Truth will require this.

Religious educators who seek to be accountable, then, will have four tasks:

1) To discover to whom they will be accountable in the parish and (probably) in the diocese.
2) To discover whether these people are ready for their account-ability.
3) To delineate carefully the area of their work for which they can be honestly accountable.
4) To avoid carefully overly operationalized terms of account-ability and insist instead on insightful, subjective measures of evaluation. Such measures might be the attitude of the students in the CCD class, the cooperation of the parents in parent-programs, the spirit of participation at Sunday liturgy, the concern for justice manifested in conversations in the teachers' lounge.

A PRACTICAL APPROACH

For the past year this writer has been at work on the problem of evaluation and accountability in the average American parish, working under the direction and with the financial support of the National Conference of Diocesan Directors of Religious Education-CCD to produce a program based on the following principles. (1) Accountability is to the parish, the community of faith called together by God in this place for this era of history. Further accountability is indeed owed to the wider church and to the Lord. But until the parish is accountable to itself it cannot meet these other terms. The research shows clearly that the initiator of the accountability-evaluation program must discover who are the real decision-makers in the parish. With a combination of these decision-makers and some of the people-in-the-pew, the evaluation is made. It is they who must be led to be accountable to themselves and to the Spirit of God who is in their midst. (2) The leadership must be ready for such accountability. It will involve them. It will undoubtedly require changes in the manner in which they operate, for accountability is a dialogue involving changes on all sides. (3) Insistence on program evaluation, not on faith formation, orthodoxy or behavior of students. Research into management theory clearly reveals that no one can be held accountable—nor hold himself or herself accountable—for that which he or she cannot control. (4) The terms of the accountability and its companion evaluation must be insightful and subjective rather than concrete and empirical. A study of the history of the church reveals that undue emphasis on the operational leads to hypocrisy and phariseeism.

A report on this project was made to the NCDD at its national meeting last Spring, and the instrument is now being field-tested in several parishes. After a final revision, the whole program will be presented to the NCDD at its meeting in the Spring of 1976. Parishes wishing to make use of the program in its incomplete stage can obtain copies from their diocesan directors.

To conclude: Sister Mary of Holy Sincerity is a good religious educator. To be an accountable one, however, she will need more than sincerity. She will need a sense of politics, a nose for power, and a willingness to work in a sticky situation, the exact limits of which have yet to be defined. She will also need to keep in mind that while accountability is a good thing, it is not the main work of religious education.

This article first appeared in PACE in 1975. The author, WILLIAM V. COLEMAN, is president of Growth Associates, an organization offering workshops for teachers and leaders, teen experiences, and consultation and resources in religious education (P. O. Box 20126, Tallahassee, Florida 32304).

4
First Communion and First Penance— A Spotcheck of Practices and Attitudes

Janet M. Bennett

In 1969, when I last took an organized look at First Communion and First Penance, it was the era of protest demonstrations and peace marches and of patches and Indian headbands and Afros and dashikis. Religion texts were similarly energetic and diversified— with glaring kodachromes and cartoons and graffiti, with role-playing, banners, balloons and torn-paper collages, and talk of our Jewish heritage, of meals and celebrations and covenants. Now six years later, both in the outside world and in religious education, many of these divergent elements have been absorbed into the system and tamed—or discarded altogether. In talks with a number of individuals, a more orderly and businesslike approach emerges. Summaries of several of these interviews follow. Though they by no means constitute a scientific sample, they do suggest something of today's range of thought.

1) The layman in charge of curriculum and catechist formation at a diocesan religious education center gave me a thorough overview of the prevailing philosophy and practices as recommended by the diocese. He and other staff members involved with sacramental preparation try to engineer the big shift in parental thinking from the fill-up-at-the-gas-station, make-me-holy-to-get-to-heaven notion to the idea that the prime responsibility of Catholics (a newer shift—the sixties called them Christians) is to continue Jesus' work as part of a community. Whereas penance once suggested erasing stains of sin which made you unworthy for heaven, now you come to the community, with your weaknesses, for help in living your life. Learning and teaching ("catechesis") should be continuous, through all the grades and all of life, not just a one-shot project with the third-grade teacher. Parents are expected to be totally involved with the process. Mandatory parent meetings are part of the plan. If parents don't participate, there's serious doubt about permitting the child to receive the sacraments. For sacraments to have meaning, they must be grounded in the child's everyday experience. "Spirit-filled prudential judgment" may, however, be applied to individual situations. If parents want their child to receive the sacraments

but they themselves refuse to attend the compulsory meetings, the child may be permitted to do so if he or she shows recognition of the importance of it all—but not "just because all the other kids are doing it."

But further, these parent meetings serve as a means of adult education, of bringing the church's new thinking to those who may still operate from an outdated base. The booklets or the ubiquitous dittos are meant to add to the parents' understanding and development, but are not intended for direct parent/child teaching. This is another shift from the early change-years when the idea of parent-as-primary-teacher was taken more literally. Then parents were expected to instruct their own children, turning to religious educators for direction and materials. Now educating the parents is seen as the way to help them towards the kind of responsible Christian living which is their obligation, and which will provide the proper atmosphere for the children's moral and spiritual growth.

Audiovisuals and the like are used less than they were five years ago. Teaching continues to be "experiential," but there is not as much game-playing, records, or singing as in the exuberant sixties. Though learning is ongoing, for both Catholic schools and CCD there are extra out-of-school classes specifically for sacraments. For this "immediate catechesis" there are separate supplementary texts, while the "remote catechesis" of the regular religion class includes materials related to sacraments as part of the everyday work. Sadlier and Benziger continue to be the standbys, with the more demanding Silver-Burdett series offered to those parishes willing to do the extra work involved. The TeleKETICS films on Eucharist and Penance remain top choices, with **No Man Is an Island**, an Orson Welles narration of John Donne's poem, a new front-runner. The latter shows the need to become involved in the sufferings of the poor, the handicapped, the aged, and reinforces the emphasis on the interrelatedness of the whole community. The new Twenty-third Publications filmstrips (**Sinner Sam, Worshipping Wilma**, etc.) are used for brief and bright presentations of the historical development of the sacraments.

The liberal-conservative split, so much talked about in recent years, appears most strongly in the question of penance-before-communion. Rome has mandated that the two sacraments be separated in time, but traditional Catholics with their residual sin-and-condemnation attitude may insist that penance come first. Since six weeks of immediate instruction for each sacrament are required, children whose parents insist on penance-first run the risk of missing out on receiving communion with their own class. Though theoretically parents have the final choice, when faced with this dilemma, "Most of them opt for doing it our way, communion first."

The communion ceremony itself offers many options: A single child at a home mass; a single child at any regularly scheduled parish mass, with the celebrant introducing the child to the community and the parents perhaps doing some of the readings (though there can be as much or as little participation as the parents want); a small group such as the children of one neighborhood; or the usual whole class. In church ceremonies, however, the child is expected to sit with his or her parents; the "performance-procession" may be preferred and may be done, but the recommended family-centered focus of the sacrament must be maintained. If there are problems which would cause embarrassment for parents who are reluctant to receive communion, these can be handled in a variety of ways, even to having the priest pretend to give communion to a parent who does not wish to be conspicuously absent from the altar rail.

"Past problems haven't been with our theology but with our sociology. Changes in our culture influence our understanding of theology." Some of these changes are presented to parents by way of humorous materials like George Carlin's "I Was an Irish Catholic" and "The Confessional" from the album **Class Clown** ("You had to **wanna**—in fact **wanna** was a whole big sin in itself—Thou Shalt Not Wanna!"), or reading of selected passages from **The Last Catholic in America**, by Powers.

2) My next visit was to the principal of religious education in a parish about thirty-five miles from New York, in a stable town of city commuters, small businesses, and workers in the several large local factories. The church membership is chiefly a mixture of Irish, Italian, and Slovak. Here there is a strong feeling that the rather purist diocesan procedures have to be adapted to the way of life of "our people," though "we've been very careful to follow all the guidelines." Parent meetings are **not** mandatory as a condition for the child's participation in the sacraments, though the parents are expected to be practicing Catholics. With a choice of evening or morning meetings (two years required of both parents and children regardless of when they begin) there is 99 percent attendance. These meetings are informal and tend to be both social and educational. Many of the parents report back that they enjoy them: "They put a whole new slant on things."

Both the school and the CCD use Sadlier throughout, with support from a large collection of parish-owned A-V materials including **This Sunday Party** and **The Little Grain of Wheat**. Parents receive mimeographed sheets, some drawn from Fides' **Things Go Better with Peace** and other backup materials from **It Is the Lord,** by Bausch, the Benziger program and others. The Twenty-third Publications filmstrip, **The First Shall Be Last,** and the new **Sin and Reconciliation** are shown to parents. Friendship, forgiveness, loving, celebration, and community are key themes; old ideas ("fish, mass, sex") are compared with these newer concerns.

Behavior is important here; parents are told that if there is any trouble or vandalism the children are to be kept at home. Teachers are advised to "worry about the children in front of you; your job is to teach, not to babysit." Behavior is also emphasized in the mimeographed examination of conscience for the children. Among the more spiritual questions are such items as: "Can I stop watching TV and play and willingly go to bed on time so I am able to work well the next day?" and "Do I enjoy gym and play games with all my heart?"

For this tradition-bound community, the hands-down preference is for the children to sit together up front in their white dresses and veils and Sunday suits. An occasional child may receive communion alone at a regular mass but this isn't common; a few ask for home masses. There are two penance services on a given Saturday which the parents and children attend together. "The climate has really changed—there's no fear at all, even of the box."

3) Next I visited a parish in one of the more affluent suburbs, close to colleges and universities and populated by corporation-related families. Here the director of religious education has spent the past four years in developing a style which is strongly tied to a philosophy of parish ministry. As in the first parish, there is a real sense of the importance of the parish's own identity. The way of life in this community is seen as a particular concern: "The younger people don't have a strong operative base. Fathers travel, mothers have social obligations related to the father's professional situation, etc. The parents are mostly very good—they want to do what's right —but they're bogged down with time and outside demands."

Religious education is thought of in terms of the whole family, with a lot of personal contact. There are parish activities, an adult lecture series, group discussions and seminars—but there's also an attempt to find ways to "feed into families without demanding that the family come out. We're trying to develop small bonds—coffees and things like that—where the instruction is only incidental." The sacraments are an avenue to ongoing growth. "If sacraments are only for ceremony or only a method of control, then we're going backward." Parent meetings are important, but every means is offered to help parents in their own circumstances. "If they can't come, we'll go to them. At least we feel we should have been in contact with the families in some way before the child receives the sacraments." The same titles appear here as elsewhere: Twenty-third Publications' **Communion: Between Parent, Teacher and Child**, from which dittos are made; the Sadlier texts, TeleKETICS films, and a new filmstrip series for second grade, **Children of Light**, from Roa. The same themes—community, friendship, loving, forgiveness, celebration and service—prevail.

4) So far things have been relatively straightforward, with the various trends of the past few years becoming stabilized in more or less similar methods and ceremonies, and fairly common philosophical principles. Each of the three individuals is enthusiastic and optimistic. Though all speak of training the lay people to take more initiative and more responsibility, even at the loosest the role of organized religious education is taken for granted as essential. A variety of options is mentioned by all three, with rather more flexibility in the parishes than in the diocesan office, reflecting what are felt to be important and inviolable community lifestyles.

But I went on with my interviewing, for one final session. This time I sat in on a morning coffee visit with two over-forty mothers (six children including several teenagers; one mother has a six-year-old and is therefore again in line for First Communion planning). These mothers live in a large, fast-growing community with many new housing developments, new schools, and civic activities. There follow some verbatim remarks made by the two women as they considered their present stand on religious education and the church and theology, and as they riffled through some of the paper and book materials I had collected on previous interviews:

"I'd like to take my own little girl—and do what **I** want—and think that I'm responsible enough and respected enough to do it my own way. By the time people reach thirty or forty and have been going to communion and experiencing life they must be at least as authoritative about what First Communion means as the teachers —maybe more so. I suppose I mean **thinking** people, of course— like every other thing in life this has to be individualized."

"Don't they believe what they used to tell us about grace? I've been **experiencing** this sacrament for thirty years or more. Doesn't it seem as though they're **saying** the grace words but just to be on the safe side they have to control the explanation too?"

"I'm deeply resentful of anything compulsory—it's very demeaning. When Lynn made her first communion, they told me that if I didn't come she couldn't receive. So I had to go and watch that absolutely asinine filmstrip, dreadfully dumb—while Lisa [her retarded daughter] crawled around under everybody's feet making her weird noises. I just didn't have anybody to leave her with. And Sister tried to tell us we had all kinds of wrong thoughts about the sacraments and the church had all kinds of new thoughts—but what she was telling us made absolutely no sense at all. Besides, does the church really have the power to refuse anyone sacraments, even a child? Who owns the sacraments anyway?"

"I **don't** think it's good for kids to be analyzing their experience this way—can't they just live? And go along with their families and take part in what their families think is important. Mommy and Daddy think this is a good thing to do, maybe with some explanation that it had to do with Jesus, and maybe something about spiritual food if they can comprehend it. Some limited ideas like you do with the Christmas story . . ."

[Reading]: "'Jesus helped at home . . .' Awful! 'God loves you for the special things you do . . .' Not true! God loves you because you're you. I wouldn't let Stephanie look at any of this stuff. Since we already have this dreadful experience of teaching in our own past, I should think they'd be less willing to make the same kind of mistake again. This stuff seems bent on hiding Christ instead of revealing him."

"Don't they realize the hatreds at this age? I don't think it's a good thing to preach forgiveness at this age—and drag Jesus into it. They should just work it through naturally—that's enough for little kids to cope with."

"I think 'alone with God' was a very noble concept. It's very comforting to a small child. Isn't life bad enough in groups nowadays—school's a whole big **mess** of a group—without making Eucharist a group thing too?"

"Don't the kids get enough of this busy-work paper stuff in school anyway? Me too—more junk paper to be responsible for. I don't have room in the house for all this stuff. There's a lot of cutesy stuff here—looks nice—but the philosophy behind it is terrible."

"They give you options? Well, I don't think they present these options too openly. I never hear about them. Anyway, if there are 'circumstances' then you're in a defensive position. You have to explain and reveal your life and reasons. Why can't they take you at face value as an adult whether you are or not? They expect us to do that for them. Some people just aren't all that well. And some people just can't **take** groups any more. I think that's perfectly legitimate all by itself. We're all overgrouped and over-stimulated nowadays. Maybe that's one of our real problems, as much a problem as these dramatic, cliché 'involvement' problems in these books and films. **The** poor. **The** handicapped. And here's me—with Lisa—but **I** have to come to meetings."

"I've gotten to the point where I don't want ceremony anyway. And people have different needs at different times. Like my sister Doris—she used to be into everything, but now with all their sickness and problems, she says she's just going to withdraw into her house and family and the heck with everybody for awhile. You know, we're supposed to be ministering to people and building the kingdom and all—but sometimes it's like a Pogo-paraphrase: 'I have met my neighbor and he is me.' We've got to **do** stuff, but we're not in shape to do it."

One final comment came from my daughter Martha, who is eighteen, as she looked over the collected sacrament materials I'd unloaded onto the kitchen table: "This stuff is horrid. What was wrong with the way we learned it—all about Mary and the saints and people back then. What was wrong with that?"

Conclusion

Though most religious educators beg off on the words "liberal" and "conservative" now, it's not hard to tell in talking with them that they regard themselves generally as the progressives of the church, gathering up and synthesizing the liberal thought of recent years and bringing it home to the people, who still lag behind. With reference to real hard-core conservative thinkers—those who don't easily tolerate ambiguity or variety—religious educators are indeed progressive. But as extensions and representatives of a large, inevitably cautious institution, religious educators are themselves conservative vis-á-vis a lot of other members of society. Many religious educators are aware of this; they often are frustrated and manage the tensions of their position only with difficulty.

Here, with the sacraments, the tension may be felt quite clearly, because aside from the spiritual function of the sacraments, it's here that the membership is visible, where it makes its pledges of allegiance and stands up to be counted. Religious education attempts to further evolutionary processes of consciousness-changing, but even today thoroughly independent thinkers really cannot be very well accommodated. The problems of the individual versus the group, and of progressive, independent thought versus group conformity and control will probably persist, especially with respect to the sacraments. The emphasis on a concept like "community" as a theological principle reflects this insistence on group identity which is increasingly important to a church and a time period which have undergone such strain. A more secure earlier church could afford to say "Dare to be different" and caution against going along with the crowd. Here is one evidence, as I heard in the first interview, that culture does indeed influence theology.

This article first appeared in PACE in 1975. The author, JANET M. BENNETT, who served as librarian for the Religious Education Office in Paterson, New Jersey, and edited **Viewpoints,** is at present a freelance writer.

5
A Team Dreams

Richelle Pearl Koller

"Team ministry," "staff meetings," "team planning," "goal setting," "priorities" are concepts in the religious education coordinator's vocabulary these days. What is not so common perhaps, are models for effective team planning and management.

Recently our staff held a two-day planning and dream session about what the ideal contemporary Christian parish might be. The format we followed, while not **the** model, might be helpful to those interested in long-range planning sessions.

After some discussion we settled on a two-fold purpose to the meeting: to assess the strengths and weaknesses of the parish in its present structure; and to determine the direction of the parish in the immediate future. With these as our goals, it was clear to us that the major thrust of the planning session was to be in the direction of task, as opposed to those planning sessions devoted to personal growth and inter-staff communication. We weighed the pros and cons of hiring a professional consultant to work with us, but decided that there was adequate leadership within the staff to build an agenda and to conduct a workshop suited to our specific needs. And so, away from the interruptions of the office, we proceeded to plan and dream about our parish and its potential.

Prior to the meeting each participant prepared a written statement of his or her personal assessment of the strengths and weaknesses of the parish. As each team member had had a different perspective and historical involvement with the parish, no prescribed outline was used for this evaluation. Rather each person was asked to reflect on the parish and its activities as he or she perceived them. The result of this assessment served as the content of our opening meeting in which we examined such areas as liturgy, education, social apostolate, parishioners, finances, staff, and parish organizations. A recurring theme that came through in the analysis of each of these areas was that as a staff we were too competent and assumed too much leadership. Consequently we were not developing the leadership potential latent within our parish community.

Following this analysis of the parish we began what we termed our "dream session." Twenty minutes of the two-hour period was set aside for each person to write a one paragraph description of his or her dream of a contemporary Christian parish. In groups of three we met to share these "visions" and then the entire staff joined in a discussion of how our parish could come closer to this ideal. It is difficult to summarize that session; such a barrage of ideas emerged. Basically we agreed that the church is a community of believers who share a common faith in a God who loves human beings in Jesus, the sign of this love. The church is those who adhere to Jesus in discipleship and apostleship. The parish is the concretization of this belief in worship and service to the needy both within and without the parish. In the parish the parishioners, not the staff, are most important. The staff is subordinate to the needs of the people and functions as a facilitator in enabling the community to realize itself as the church in the best sense of the term, through ministry and service. The staff is servant of the community enabling the members of the community to identify with an enduring Christian tradition, bringing that tradition into focus for today and orienting the community toward life in contemporary society.

From this dreaming or blue-skying we began to determine our priorities. Each staff member in our next session drew up four specific goals for the coming year listing the positive and negative resources available for achieving each goal. Again we shared these, first in small groups and then as a total staff. After a long discussion we came to an agreement on the four goals that would in the year ahead help move us toward our dream. These goals were:

1) To establish a parish liturgy commission so as to involve the parishioners in planning the prayer life of the parish.
2) To develop a social action committee that would work to involve the parish in the needs of the metropolitan community.
3) To take a parish census so as to discover the potential within the parish.
4) To work on inter-staff communication and role-clarification.

The final session of our planning meeting was spent outlining procedures, establishing a time-table, assigning responsibilities and determining the means of evaluating our progress toward the accomplishment of these goals. We left the two-day workshop more united as a staff, more conscious of the meaning of church, more aware of our priorities and clearer in our understanding of the direction of the coming year. Already we see many ways of improving our planning session, but for the moment we have begun, we have dreamed, we have seen blue-sky.

STAFF SEMINAR AGENDA
First Day

3:00 p.m. Sharing of the Assessment of the Strengths and Weaknesses of the Parish.

5:00   Social hour and supper

7:30   Dream Session. The first twenty minutes spent individually. Then a forty-five minute sharing session in small groups.

8:30   Entire staff discussion of the Christian Parish. The meeting terminated about 10:00 p.m.

Second Day

9:15 a.m. Goal setting. First done individually, then as a small group.

10:00   Staff discussion of goals, establishing of priorities for the year.

11:30   Lunch

2:00   Finalization session. In light of the morning's work on common goal setting and analysis of resources and hindering forces, the strategies for achieving the goals together with means of evaluation should be determined. This is to be done first in small groups, then shared with the entire staff. Staff members participating in the session were the pastor, his two associates, the grade school principal, the religious education coordinator, and two CCD staff members.

This article first appeared in PACE in 1972. The author, RICHELLE PEARL KOLLER, is presently religious education coordinator for Christ the King Parish in Minneapolis. She holds her M.A. in religious education from SUMORE, Seattle University.

6
Understanding Church Organization

Christine Long

Five years ago I began to work as a professional in religious education. I wanted to contribute to the renewal of parish life and the renovation of the church. I assumed success would follow from an adequate theology, competence, hard work, and good will.

I don't believe that any more.

Don't misunderstand. I'm not trying to get off the hook. There are minimum standards of honest professionalism. But I'm pragmatist enough to admit that theology, skill, labor, and concern neither cause nor explain success in pastoral work. They have not always been absent in disasters, nor present when things went well.

But—as I said—I'm pragmatic. I don't like to suffer unexplained guilt when things don't go well. I lose motivation when every task has an unpredictable outcome. I dislike meetings where everyone is speaking in a different code. So I started looking for a more encompassing explanation of what goes on in the parish. The need was crystallized one night after I had attended a series of five planning sessions for the high school religion program. I had an uncomfortable sense that it was all useless—the kids wouldn't want what had been planned. As I was telling my husband about it, I blurted out a bone-truth—and I heard what I said—"It won't work and it's not supposed to. The program is **organized** to fail!"

Sometime later I joined a group of church workers of several denominations led by Dr. Robert C. Worley of McCormick Theological Seminary in Chicago. We looked at the way the church functions **as an organization**. Our work proved invaluable to me. It clarified my future plans as a professional religious educator. It gave me some needed tools for planning and executing programs in the church. I would like to share some of our theory and exercises with you.

Most of us have been operating from a personal and relational model of faith. We've also been polishing our human relations skills. That has been necessary. It remains essential. But I believe that we can't exercise that faith or those skills unless organizational structures offer a favorable environment for them. No one has ever become neurotic because the worship, preaching, and teaching in their church is less than excellent. But many people have been driven into sickness by the shape of the organization to which they belong. I believe that there is a direct relationship between the kind of organization that exists and the type of behavior that results (and the sorts of people who assign themselves to the organization). Let me illustrate that through an exercise you can do with a group.

EXERCISE 1:
COMMUNICATION PATTERNS AND THEIR EFFECTS

Structure:
Twenty-five participants are needed for this exercise. It can be adapted to a smaller number of people as long as there are five members in each group-pattern. Some of the group-patterns may be dropped, or some may be used on one occasion and the rest at another time.

Aim of the Exercise:
This exercise is designed to show the effects of different patterns of communication: (1) on persons while they are members of a group; (2) on the process of accomplishing the group-goal; and (3) on the nature of the organization itself.

Method:
Persons may hear and speak to others in their group **only** as indicated by the arrows on their group pattern.

Group-Patterns:

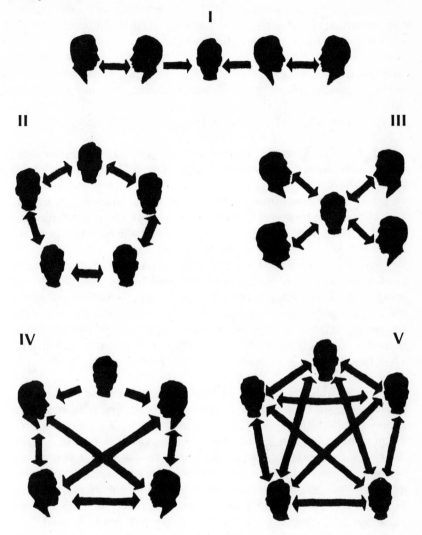

Time:
45 minutes for discussion of the problem; 45 minutes for feedback on the problem and analysis of the process.

Group-Goal:
To develop an **agreement** on the problem set out below.

Problem:
To decide what is the most significant or critical difficulty facing
the organization to which the participants belong (parish, staff,
etc.) and develop a strategy for meeting it.

Analysis of the Process:
Some suggestive questions to consider during the analysis of the
process:

1) Leadership: Who thought they had it? Who took it? Who
   refused to consent? Why?
2) Accuracy of communication: Were you confident your ideas
   were considered? Were you able to consider the ideas of the
   others in your group?
3) Goal-accomplishment: Were you able to reach agreement?
4) Describe how you felt about the persons (a) with whom you
   had interchange, (b) who you could hear but not speak to,
   (c) who you could speak to but not hear.

Structure causes a different group-character in each design.
Consensus, for example, is never achieved in any but a Group V
design. The individuals in the other designs may have many group
skills, but they cannot exercise them and come to agreement save
by accident. What is even more surprising is that those individuals
behave in ways characteristic to their positions in the group design.
They may be hostile or apathetic because of where they sit!

This exercise represents communication patterns that appear
in **every** parish. Does that seem farfetched? At first it would seem
that only the Group V pattern is common—discussion groups at least
claim to follow it. But the other designs also exist in the real world.
For example, Group I could be the parish. Imagine that you are an
"ordinary" parishioner—you're in the middle position. You keep
getting messages but you have no influence on the message-givers.
Eventually you rebel and refuse cooperation. If you imagine yourself
to be one of the message-givers, your position is not improved. You
are in competition for the parishioner's attention with someone
else. You can exchange conversation with one other person. But you
resent that person after several attempts to relay his or her messages to your unresponsive audience. Or suppose you are in one of
the end positions. You might feel that you are the leader of the
group. After all, you can ask that the word be passed along. But you
know that someone else is doing the same thing at the other end of
the line. He or she might be undercutting you.

Suppose now that you are a DRE whose job-situation places

you into a Group-III-like operation. You are in the middle—and harried. The messages keep coming in and going out. You have no time to plan a strategy. You realize that it appears that you have a lot of power. But even Machiavelli couldn't exercise power without leisure. You don't even have time to notice that the participants are bored and apathetic: they must wait too long to communicate.

Finally look at Group IV and imagine that the pastor of the parish is in the isolated position. He is able to speak only to the principal of the parochial school and the coordinator of the CCD. But he can't hear from them. He talks more and more. And they listen to him less and less. They react with hostility when he interrupts their conversations with others. In time they become suspicious of each other.

Every attempt to communicate generates tension. My metabolism is raised by the pressure of putting myself up-front, of trying to get a message across, of adapting to the ideas of others. Tasks can be accomplished by harnessing that tension. But that is true only if there is a match between the goal and the technology to reach the goal. Otherwise tension is destructive. People become hostile or apathetic, suspicious or bored. And the goal cannot be reached.

In a sense, the exercise was stacked. The goal (reaching agreement) and the technology (all could interchange) were congruent only in Group V. Only that design made members accountable for their views, allowed leadership to shift according to competence, and let the group know when it had succeeded. But had the task been different, another design would have been "right" and other criteria of success would be applied. Suppose the task had been to record the opinions of several smaller groups. The Group I design would have worked. Or that you, as a DRE, wanted to inform teachers of a session cancellation. Group II or Group III would have done the job. The tension generated by the effort to communicate would then flow—as it should—into task-accomplishment.

This article first appeared in PACE in 1971. The author, CHRISTINE LONG, is a freelance writer and consultant in religious education who studied at McCormick Theological Seminary. She has been a parish DRE and diocesan staff member. She lives in North Riverside, Illinois, with her husband, Jerome, and three children.

Counsel from the Field

7
Internship for DREs

Mary Margaret Funk

In September of 1975, the Archdiocese of Indianapolis sponsored a symposium entitled "What is the Ministry of a DRE?" It was discovered at this symposium that the ministry of the Director of Religious Education is being shaped by the DREs themselves, the parishes and people to whom they minister, and other influences such as colleges and diocesan offices. One concern regarding this ministry was seen to be the initiation of prospective DREs into this new profession. Internship was suggested as one means of addressing this concern. Now, two years later, we are still working on models and details for an internship program in this diocese.

At the present time, the Office of Catholic Education makes these recommendations regarding internship: (1) that every person graduating with a B.A. in Religious Education have at least one semester of an internship practicum; (2) that teachers who switch from teaching into religious education administration have a nine-week period of internship with a professional DRE before applying for a full-time DRE position; (3) that each parish hiring a first-year DRE give an applicant who has not participated in an internship program a lower base salary than one who is an experienced intern; (4) that each college with a Religious Education major offer an internship practicum in both teaching and administration.

In most cases, the student makes a connection through the diocesan office with a parish willing to take him/her. Sometimes, however, the student uses his/her home parish, and connections can be made directly between its DRE and the student. Internships are designed to fit the needs of each individual student/applicant. For example, college credits are given by St. Mary-of-the-Woods College in St. Mary-of-the-Woods, Indiana, for internship in a parish, usually under the supervision of a professional DRE. Contracts stating specific experience requirements are worked out between the faculty supervisor and the student, and specific learning experiences are outlined with the DRE. When a DRE is not involved in the internship, the faculty supervisor aids the student in the development of the specific program.

WHY INTERNSHIP?

Internship is not only useful for the prospective DRE as a career preparation, but is also helpful to the diocesan office, the college that prepares DREs, and the parish that hires the DRE. A diocesan office finds internship helpful because the process of designing a program of internship forces a focus on the role of a DRE. It is a chance to observe several personalities and styles of leadership at work in the same parish. This helps us to answer the question, "Who works best and with whom?"

Colleges benefit from the internship program because it is a checkpoint for outcomes. It helps them answer the question, "Does what we offer in the curriculum assist the prospective DRE to be effective in the parish?" One can argue that knowledge is not directly applicable in practice, but today we are making the colleges responsible for providing the students with usable skills and ideas. Learning is broader than conceptual knowledge.

Parishes also need to be a part of the evolution of a professional in religious education. The internship affords parish personnel the opportunity to dialogue with the prospective DRE as a peer, letting him/her know what ought to be his/her role before being hired. The conversation between the board member and/or the pastor and the DRE before he/she has the status of being an employee offers a free exchange. Other parishes can watch the prospective DRE and his/her work in the internship and invite him/her to work in their parish as a paid professional.

A recommendation comes from either the college, the pastor, or the diocesan office of education after the prospective DRE has been seen at work on the parish level. All three—the parish, the college, and the diocesan office—need to provide the prospective DRE with the experience, the background, and the credentials which will help him/her do the task. Internship is one focal point in the process of shaping this new profession in the church.

WHAT WOULD AN INTERNSHIP LOOK LIKE?

An internship should consist of: actual teaching experiences with children and adults; the experience of planning and implementing a specific program and reporting the progress and outcome to the board; participating in meetings of the pastoral team; gathering the resources necessary to conduct at least one project such as a teacher training session, a special liturgy, or a sacramental preparation program; and the opportunity to examine the current text used in the school or CCD. The intern should hear why each text is effective and how the DRE assists each teacher to maximize the effectiveness of each book at each age level and in family programs. The process of the internship should be a mini-experience in the total process of being a DRE. The prospective DRE should learn to set goals with objectives that can be measured and evaluated.

HOW CAN INTERNSHIP BE PROMOTED?

A salary scale could give an increment for those first-year DREs who have had internship compared with those who have not had this experience. Secondly, those who take the internship should receive a higher or more credible recommendation that is recognized by the parishes that hire. In addition, the boards that write up the description of need for the parish could state a preference for those persons having had internship experience.

In conclusion, this Office of Catholic Education promotes internship for DREs because we believe that the profession of Director of Religious Education is too important to take unnecessary chances for failure, such as placing an inexperienced person in a parish. Even Jesus insisted that the Apostles have an internship in ministry before he sent them out in pairs to proclaim the Kingdom and to minister to those in need.

This article first appeared in PACE in 1977. The author, SISTER MARY MARGARET FUNK, OSB, is director of the Department of Religious Education in the Office of Catholic Education of the Archdiocese of Indianapolis.

8
The Coordinator and the Parish: A Hiring Process

Gregory Presnail

Over the course of the last half-decade, a growing number of parishes across the nation have made the decision to hire a coordinator or director of religious education. Based on the financial condition of most parishes, the decision has not been made casually. But too often the search and hiring process following the decision has been far too casual. The result is that the coordinator and the parish, both acting in good faith, find themselves in the course of the association, at best, disappointed and, at worst, embittered.

The intent of this article is to provide help both to parishes and to coordinators in their mutual assessment.

SELF-DIAGNOSIS

Before a parish can intelligently begin to search for a coordinator, it has a number of tasks to perform. The most fundamental is basically diagnostic, not unlike the physician's question, "Where does it hurt?" The parish has to make some assessments of its strengths and weaknesses with regard to religious education. Existing programs have to be examined individually since the same weaknesses are not necessarily common to them all. Often needs will fall into general categories. These categories would include, but not necessarily be confined to, theology, methodology, organization, and administration.

Those who are most directly involved in the programs can be expected best to identify their strengths and weaknesses. The evaluators would include pastor, teachers, program administrators, and parents. This kind of broad consultation provides helpful data and, beyond that, begins to build the base of support a new coordinator needs for effective service.

The next step is to consolidate the data and to categorize the weaknesses, initially identified. Once this is done the parish has some orderly data to act upon.

Continuing the earlier analogy, this process is much like the physician's effort to localize the problem. In clinical terms he or she might ask, "Where does it hurt most?" The parish should begin localizing the problem by rating its needs, and concentrating on those judged to be most important, deferring consideration of those needs considered unimportant or trivial.

The reason for this process is that applicants for the position of coordinator have their own set of competencies. The applicant's education, experience, and interests can be superbly appropriate for one parish and completely inappropriate for another. For example, if a parish concludes that the area of greatest need is the organization and administration of its programs, it would be tragic if it hired a highly creative, skillful, resourceful teacher who regularly wore unmatched shoes.

The other caution is that few persons have professional educational competencies to deal with all levels from pre-school through adult education. A person whose professional experience has been confined to elementary education cannot be expected to be equally competent with a high school program (or necessarily even interested in it). This kind of expectation is naive and unfair to the coordinator and, finally, to the parish.

JOB DESCRIPTION FORMULATION

After a parish has prioritized its needs, it should translate these needs into a job description. The ideal job description identifies what the coordinator is expected to do, describes relationally how it is to be done, and leaves the coordinator room for implementation. "The coordinator will provide teacher-training programs for elementary religious education teachers" is not as helpful as "The coordinator will, in consultation with the elementary religious education teachers, design and implement teacher training programs responsive to their needs." The latter phrasing protects the parish from undesirable autocratic service. It also protects the coordinator by making the teacher training a shared responsibility.

The next task is to develop a budget. The budget should include: salary, fringe benefits (both those required by law and those customarily provided by employer), office expenses (capital as well as operating), secretarial services, professional expenses, and program budgets. Housing expenses should be included if the applicant is a religious. Ideally, the budget should have some flexibility.

PARISH PROFILE

A prospective coordinator will obviously be interested in knowing as much as possible about the parish. For this reason, data should be provided regarding its size (geographic as well as population), setting, age distribution, educational levels, ethnic character, parochial school size and grades, and any other descriptive information. This profile sheet, as well as the job description, should be mailed to the applicant as soon as the job request is received.

THE SEARCH

The diocesan office should be advised that there is an opening in your parish. Contact should be made not only with the religious serving your parish but also with those serving the diocese generally. Graduate schools should be alerted. Neighboring parishes should be contacted. Ads may be placed quite inexpensively in diocesan or in national newspapers.

Applicants, as a rule, will include references as part of their resume. **These references should be contacted**. If the information they provide is ambiguous or vague, phone these persons for clarification.

Some applicants will obviously be ill-suited for the position. You owe them the courtesy of a letter acknowledging their interest and advising them (in the politest of terms) that they don't fill your requirements. It is extremely unfair and discourteous to ignore any applicant.

Those who do appear acceptable should be contacted immediately. The quickest and most effective way is by phone. You can thus investigate questions arising from the person's resume and the applicant can clarify areas of concern relating to your parish.

If, following the phone conversation, a mutual attraction still exists, the parish should arrange for a local interview. It is best if an applicant can spend a few days at the parish. This gives the person an opportunity to explore the parish thoroughly, talk to many people, and make a better informed decision. The parish can help the candidate by arranging the meetings with the pastor, school principal, teachers, board members, and others who can give the applicant helpful insights into the parish.

THE INTERVIEW

The interview is a directed conversation for the purpose of assessing the potentialities of an applicant as they relate to parish needs and expectations.

From the applicant's point of view, the purpose of the interview is to assess whether or not this is the parish where his/her talents and skills can best be used.

It is best to have a number of informed people participate in the interview. Each person can be expected to have insights and perceptions that will be helpful in making the final decision.

THE INTERVIEWING PROCESS

There are two schools of thought on interviewing. One proposes that the interview be structured. The same questions should be asked of each applicant. The other suggests that the interview be much freer.

The ideal falls in between. Basically, the job description should be reviewed and points should be clarified. The salary and fringe benefits and budgets should be discussed and, perhaps, negotiated. The applicant's background should be reviewed, including academic as well as professional experience.

Both parties should feel free to ask direct, probing questions as well as general, more open ones. For example, after the preliminary job description discussion, the question could be asked, "What part of the job description can you handle most competently?" Or, "What part of the job description do you most dislike?" Or, "On a scale of one to five where would you put yourself (1) representing total disorganization to (5) representing compulsive orderliness?" Or, "What would be some of the anxieties that you can foresee having if you accepted employment here?"

Additional questions might be: "Will you share with us your philosophy of education?" and "What do you regard as the most critical problem facing the church?"

The applicant has the same right to ask equally probing questions: "Outside of education, what do you see as your greatest parish problem?" "Where do you locate the greatest tensions in the parish?" "Can you describe the ideal parish religious education program?" "If you could wave a wand and change the parish, what would you change?"

The whole point of an interview is to exchange information and to determine as far as is humanly possible whether the applicant is the right person for the parish. Obviously the applicant has the same interest in the assessment of the parish. An interview where information is concealed, questions are answered deviously, facts are distorted is worse than no interview at all.

One last point. Any serious discrepancy between the information given by an applicant and information provided by a reference should be investigated.

The process just described is time-consuming, but well worth it since it diminishes to a great extent many of the hazards that contribute to the unnecessarily high turnover presently experienced in this ministry.

This article first appeared in PACE in 1974. The author, GREGORY PRESNAIL, is the coordinator consultant for the Archdiocese of St. Paul and Minneapolis.

9
Contracts in Educational Ministry

Joseph C. Neiman

With spring in the educational calendar comes the process of evaluation. The students, the programs, and the teaching personnel are scrutinized in order to plan extensions or changes for the coming academic year. While tests, questionnaires, and such are used for student and program evaluation, contract deliberations are the typical process for the evaluation of present and/or the selection of new personnel.

Religious educators, however, tend to resist signing employment contracts with a local church, feeling that such business matters are inappropriate in a Christian community. If contracts are simply routine business documents and if contract deliberations are actually negotiations wherein each party divests the other of some power or service, then such resistance is very necessary. On the other hand, if contracts can be seen in a covenant perspective, then contract deliberations can provide an opportunity for real growth in the Christian community.

WHAT IS A CONTRACT?

Legally a contract is a promise between two persons enforceable by law. Usually it is the result of a bargaining process in which one person (individual or corporate) agrees to give the one(s) making the promise something in exchange. That which is exchanged may be property, money, service or something similar. If person A promises something to person B but B gives nothing in return, the contract is termed **unilateral**. If both A and B promise something to one another, the contract is termed **bilateral**. The making of a contract requires mutual assent by both persons (parties). What is offered by one or both is stated in the terms of the contract as an expression of the promise by the parties to fulfill the exchange. Assenting to the terms of the contract means assenting to the exchange. In law only the reasonable understanding created by the terms of the contract is enforceable and not the subjective intentions of the parties. In enforcing a contract the law seeks to effect the original intention of the contracting parties by ensuring that the exchange is made or that reparation for the broken promise is given.

Contracts are the subject of a great deal of contemporary jurisprudence (law making and interpreting) mainly because we have such an elaborate system of credit or economic exchange. Contract law, however, is a rather recent development in civil jurisprudence. From the collapse of the Roman empire up until rather modern times, the Church was the main source of contract "jurisprudence" since in essence a contract is an obligation created and determined by the will of the parties involved and hence a moral matter.

Until the development of elaborate systems of credit, therefore, contracts were a personal, familial, or political matter under religious sanction. The promises were expressed orally and sealed with an oath and/or a handshake. Some were expressed in writing and formalized with the seal of the parties. Both were generally made before witnesses who could testify throughout their life as to the nature and the circumstances of the promises.

If a contract were broken, the individual exacted payment—often harshly as Matthew's gospel depicts (18:34)—or the family began a feud to seek reparation. If such private means failed, the suffering party sought justice in the court of the chancery of the Church. An adverse judgment might mean excommunication for the guilty person which effectively cut him or her off from organized society: political, economic, and religious.

The chancery courts employed clerics educated in canon law. These clerics are part of the forefathers of the legal profession.

Many a young man sought tonsure as a cleric without ordination in order to become educated, thus securing "professional status," and yet not be subject completely to the authority of the Church.

There were frequently tensions between the courts of the chancery and the courts of the palace (which handled political agreements) over jurisdiction, revenue from court fees, and the enforcement of judgments. As the power of the state increased over that of the Church, more and more of the jurisprudence pertaining to moral matters such as contracts (like marriage) were incorporated into civil courts and legislatures. Today only a vestige of the court of the chancery remains, dealing largely with matters such as marriage and promises related to religious vocations.

ARE CONTRACTS APPROPRIATE IN THE LOCAL CHURCH?

While we can see that historically the Church was quite involved with contracts, nevertheless the question of the appropriateness still remains, particularly since we are seeking to renew the structures and processes of the Church today largely in terms of biblical research.

Contracts within the Church are not exactly legal promises enforceable by law, that is civil law. Even if courts will admit cases pertaining to broken contractual agreements in the area of employment, nevertheless this avenue for due process is highly inappropriate albeit necessary in some circumstances. The real strength binding promises within the Christian community comes not from civil jurisprudence on contracts but from theological and biblical reflection on covenants.

The Hebrew word for **covenant** means a binding tie between persons. As McKenzie points out, early Hebrew society had few written agreements and hence "the spoken word was invested with ritual solemnity which gave it a kind of concrete reality" (John L. McKenzie. "Covenant." **Dictionary of the Bible**. Milwaukee: Bruce, 1965). When such spoken agreements were formalized before witnesses, they became a covenant, that is, "A solemn ritual agreement which served the function of a written contract." Strong blessings and curses flowed from the keeping or breaking of such covenanted relationships.

The constitutive elements of biblical covenants include the following: (1) the parties to the agreement, (2) the stipulations of the agreement, (3) the oaths and blessings and curses, and (4) a ritual enactment. Examples of Old Testament covenants include political alliances (Gen. 14:13; Josh. 9:15), settling of disputes (Gen. 21:31; 26:38), and friendship bonds such as that between David and Jonathan (1 Sam. 18:3).

The predominant understanding of covenant within the Bible and the Christian community, however, is that theological expression meant to explain God's relationship with the people. In the Old Testament it is the Sinai covenant (Exod. 19) between Yahweh and Israel; in the New Testament it is the Eucharist covenant (Matt. 26:28) between Christ and his disciples (Church). The principal covenant form upon which the Bible builds is the treaty pattern used by the ancient Hittites. Their treaties were of two kinds: (1) the suzerainty treaty between unequal parties such as a king and his vassals, and (2) parity treaties between equals. Suzerainty treaties were mainly unilateral whereas parity treaties were bilateral, that is, both equal parties exchanged something in order to make the contract valid.

The covenanted relationship portrayed between God and the people is unilateral since the parties were unequal and since the offer originated freely with God. To say that the covenant is unilateral, however, does not imply that God does nothing. The Scriptures clearly show that God saves the people and continually remains faithful to them even when they do not fulfill their promises. The covenant is also unilateral in the sense that there was (is) nothing which Israel (or Jesus' disciples) could do to initiate such a relationship nor to make the exchange of equal value.

Covenants, therefore, play a large role in the Christian community's self understanding. Thus ties between persons which are seen as covenants are much stronger than promises formalized into civil contracts binding in law. Hence covenant theology provides a much stronger frame of reference for understanding contracts in educational ministry.

CONTRACTS IN EDUCATIONAL MINISTRY

In light of the above, contracts in the local Church should be viewed as incarnate expressions of the call and the commissioning to ministry in the educational mission. (I use the term, "educational mission," to denote the answer which the local Church gives to the question: what should we do in education?) Beneath the economic format the Christian community is entering into a covenanted relationship with one whom the Spirit has given a charism for teaching (see 1 Cor. 12). This reality has a number of implications for contract deliberations including, it seems to me, the following:

First, contract deliberations and documents should reflect a tone of educational ministry rather than economic stipulations alone. Contracts between parishes and coordinators, for example, have little legal value anyway and hence they need not follow a tight legal format. Discussions should be in a spirit of prayerful deliberation about the educational mission of the local Church and the contributions which this person can make. This need not mean that the discussions and the documents (contracts, supplements, role descriptions, etc.) should be unreasonably vague. Both civil jurisprudence and biblical theology would teach us that the stipulations of contracts or covenants should be stated clearly albeit in broad terms. Civil contracts tend to fail most frequently where the parties express themselves obscurely, where they leave large parts of their intentions unexpressed in the terms of the agreement. "You shall not kill" (Exod. 20:13) is quite clear even though the implications of this covenant stipulation in all aspects of life are left unstated.

Secondly, both the local Church and the educational minister (coordinator, principal, teacher, etc.) should realize that the contract is a unilateral agreement parallel with the biblical covenant. The Christian community and the educational minister are not equal parties exchanging something which effects the contract. There is nothing the coordinator can do, for example, to become worthy to teach the gospel. The charism for teaching is given freely by the Spirit and is not the direct result of a degree program however designed. As Paul puts it: "No one can confess 'Jesus is Lord' unless he is guided by the Holy Spirit" (1 Cor. 12:3). Furthermore the Christian community is not being magnanimous in paying a coordinator for indeed "the Lord has directed that those who preach the gospel should get their living from it" (1 Cor. 9:14).

Thirdly, realizing that the contract is a unilateral covenant between the Christian community and the minister of the gospel should bring both parties to a deeper awareness of the demands of fidelity which signing this symbolic document expressed. Both must realize, for example, that the Christian community is founded upon the cornerstone of Jesus Christ and is not a creation built around either a Church dogma or a theological theory. "We are simply God's servants" (1 Cor. 3:5). Hence whatever either the local Church or the coordinator does must be done "in the name of the Lord Jesus" (Col 3:17). As Paul says: "There are different ways of serving but the same Lord is served" (1 Cor. 12:5).

In addition to the joint demands which the gospel makes upon both, there are unique demands for each. The local Church must be faithful to the minister of the Word much like Yahweh with Israel as Hosea would teach us: supporting, sustaining, bearing patiently, and listening to the voice of the Spirit which may come through this person whom the Spirit has endowed with spiritual gifts. The local Church, therefore, must not "play with" educational ministers, keeping them around for token tasks until they are no longer needed. Rather a genuine sharing of the ministry of teaching the gospel must be part of the commissioning in the contract.

On the other hand the coordinator (principal, teacher, etc.) must also realize that the charism of teaching is freely given by the Spirit for the building up of the assembly of believers. Furthermore, it is the community—not the professional, nor the diocesan office, nor an organization—which discerns whether the charism is for the good of all. "Since you are eager to have the gifts of the Spirit," Paul admonishes, "above everything else you must try to make greater use of those which help build up the Church" (1 Cor. 14:12). In practical terms this demands a prayerful effort to discern which of the ideas and programs proposed are of "God's wisdom" and for the benefit of the community; and which are of "man's wisdom" and incapable of teaching spiritual truths.

Lastly it would seem that understanding contracts in the local Church as covenanted relationships would necessitate ritual enactment rather than mere routine signing. When the parish and the coordinator, for example, have come to a consensus about the contract, then a public liturgical celebration would be most appropriate. This celebration would emphasize (1) the basic responsibility of all believers for communicating the gospel through a symbolic endorsement of the responsibilities of parents and communal bodies such as educational boards and committees; (2) the special commissioning of the various persons who have been called to share their teaching charism within the community in more formal ways.

In sum, contracts are indeed an important part of educational ministry, and contract deliberations provide a good opportunity for the local Church and the teaching personnel to grow spiritually mature in the "hidden wisdom of God" (1 Cor. 2:7). I realize this sounds idyllic but it seems to me that only a clear ideal such as this can help us sort through the tangle of words in contracts, job descriptions, and contract deliberations. Unless this ideal is incarnate somehow, is the educational enterprise Christian?

BIBLIOGRAPHY

Ernst Käsemann. "Ministry and Community in the New Testament."
   Essays on New Testament Themes. London: SCM Press, 1964.
John L. McKenzie. "Aspects of Old Testament Thought." **Jerome
   Biblical Commentary**. Englewood Cliffs: Prentice-Hall, 1968.
Hans Küng. "The Charismatic Structure of the Church." **The Church
   and Ecumenism**. Concilium vol. 4. New York: Paulist, 1965.
W. J. Reader. **Professional Men: The Rise of the Professional Classes
   in Nineteenth Century England.** London: Weidenfeld & Nichol-
   son, 1966.
Richard Wincor. **The Law of Contracts**. New York: Oceana Pubs.,
   1970.

(Sample "contract" for use in a ritual enactment of the local Church
follows.)

EDUCATIONAL SERVICE CONTRACT

We, the Pastor and People of _____
Parish, recognizing our mandate to "Go to the whole world and proclaim the Good News to all creation" (Mark 15:16), hereby call and
commission (name) _____
to assist us in fulfilling our educational mission as (e.g., Coordinator
of Religious Education) _____

_____

_____

We commission you to share the gifts of teaching the gospel which
the Spirit of Christ has given you and to assist us with our communal
mandate by fulfilling the responsibilities described in Supplement A
attached herewith. We implore you to be "careful always to choose
the right course; to be brave under trials; and to make the preaching
of the Good News your life's work, in thoroughgoing service" (2
Tim. 4:5).

Recognizing that "the Lord has directed that those who preach the
gospel should get their living from it" (1 Cor. 9:14), we pledge our
support and cooperation in the manner described in Supplement B
also attached herewith.

We reserve the right to discern whether the gifts which you share
are for "the common good" (1 Cor. 14:16) recognizing at the same
time that "there are many gifts but always the same Spirit" (1 Cor.
12:4) and that we are both called to be faithful to the one "Good
News of Christ" which we have all received and which can never be
changed (Gal. 1:6-9).

In all our efforts together we seek to grow spiritually mature by
"remaining faithful to the teachings of the apostles, to the community, to the breaking of the bread, and to the prayers" (Acts 2:42).

In this way we can fulfill our mandate of "making disciples of all nations" (Matt. 28:19).

In witness thereof on this the _____ in the year of our Lord _____ we affix our names:

Pastor: _____
President, Board of Education: _____
Coordinator: _____

This article first appeared in PACE in 1972. The author, JOSEPH C. NEIMAN, has been coordinator of research and development at Divine Word International Centre, author of **Coordinators** (Saint Mary's Press), and a member of a task-force for up-grading the profession of religious education coordinator.

10
Pre-Employment Approaches for DREs—Salaries and Benefits

Daryl Olszewski

THE PRESENT SITUATION

Talking about money is like talking about politics or sex. It's one of those topics which should be avoided in polite conversation. It is bound to lead to trouble, and in many cases has done so. Yet it is an area which cannot be avoided.

When one considers the compensation for the work of a DRE, one is dealing not only with a profession but also with one which happens to provide a service within and to the Church. Parishes contract with architects and builders to construct huge edifices and hire plumbers and roofers to repair leaks without looking upon these services as "service to the Church." Pastors may grumble about high prices and worry about where the money will come from, but the price is usually paid.

The low cost of ministerial services provided by priests and members of religious orders in the past has perhaps led many parish leaders, lay people included, to think that these same services should be provided by lay people at the same low cost. And perhaps this same low salary could be paid to lay people—if a house, car, meals, and retirement benefits were also provided!

Some parishes may still work from the premise that a DRE is little more than a glorified former teacher who took some summer courses in theology. Some DREs do fit this description. This type of thinking and the existence of professionally unprepared DREs cause many parishes to get away with paying a glorified teacher's salary. Extending an already low salary from ten months to twelve months gives the appearance of the parish investing a great deal "just for CCD."

What will change this situation? Time, patience, and hard work. Changing attitudes never occurs easily or quickly. Part of the problem can be resolved with the total professional preparation of DREs. Another consideration is that many pastors and parishes don't know exactly what DREs do or should be doing. Good job descriptions can help rectify this situation. DREs presently in the field may have to take the initiative to establish reporting systems to councils, education committees, and other influential groups in the parish. Once these groups realize the types and amount of services rendered by a DRE, appreciation and economic compensation may eventually follow.

One last problem is an aspect that may take a millennium to resolve. The Roman Catholic tradition is one which is steeped in reverence and devotion for the Eucharist, not the Word. It has only been since Vatican II that the Word has again been allowed to enter the mainstream of Roman Catholic life. An understanding of the Word is only beginning and, as this understanding develops and matures, so—we hope—will the appreciation and reverence for it. The ministry of a DRE is a ministry of the Word. As understanding and appreciation for the Word grows, so also might the understanding and appreciation of those who are ministers of that Word.

OBSTRUCTION TO PROCLAIMING THE KINGDOM

If a DRE is seen as a minister of the Word and this ministry involves proclaiming the Good News of the Kingdom of God in an educational setting, then nothing should interfere with or obstruct this proclamation. The statements of Jesus regarding wealth as an obstacle to entrance to the Kingdom does not presently seem to be a problem for DREs. Rather, the dictum that the laborer is worth his or her pay is the one that seems to be ignored. If concern for the cost of living, supporting a family, and the like are obstacles to a full proclamation of the Word, then this is a concern which must be resolved.

There are few people who ever have enough money for all the materials goods which they would like, just as there are few who would believe that the economy is always sound, no matter how high the GNP, how low the national debt, or which party occupies the White House. However, there are probably few, if any, who would consider ministering in the Church as a way to get rich. The point is that reasonable material resources must be made available so as not to obstruct the proclamation of the Kingdom.

REASONABLE RESOURCES

In considering compensation for the services of a DRE, one certainly has to consider the tremendous economic differences throughout the country. The cost of living may be much higher in one part of the country than in another. Even within a diocese or city, one part may be poor while another is affluent. Does this mean that a DRE should receive compensation solely on the basis of where he or she is employed? No, but it should be considered in arriving at a **reasonable** salary. **Reasonable resources** are those which do not obstruct the proclamation of the Kingdom. Each situation and individual necessities have to be evaluated to determine how much or how little will be an obstacle to this full ministerial service. It is a delicate balance to achieve.

Parishes have a duty to pay a just wage, not only for the economic well-being of the DRE, but out of justice to all the people who are served within that parish. If low salaries cause a high rate of turnover in parish personnel, the people of the parish are the ones who will suffer. It takes time for a DRE to build a relationship with a total parish and vice versa. If the low salary causes the annual departure of the DRE, then the relationship can never grow and mature. This is a relationship which is founded in the Word, and if the proclamation and growth of the Word suffers, there will probably be some reckoning on the last day.

SOME SCALES

There are a number of diocesan guidelines and salary scales for DREs. However, most of them appear to be attempts simply to organize an otherwise disorganized and inconsistent arrangement. Even if guidelines are issued, they are only useful if people follow them. Many times a DRE entering a diocese will be unaware of the guidelines, and the pastor may ignore them. That leaves the bargaining at the individual level and can only lead to a host of problems.

Diocesan scales which simply take the pay rate for teachers, even high school teachers, and adapt it to a twelve month contract help to provide consistency but detract from the actual worth of a DRE. These scales imply that a DRE is doing no more than a high school teacher, except that the work is being done for twelve months!

WHAT IS IT WORTH?

Trying to compensate a DRE for services performed is like trying to pay a housewife her full value (excuse the sexist language for this example). With a housewife one gets the services of a cook (try eating at a restaurant for a week), a laundry service (send it out to have it done once), cleaning lady (good help is hard to find these days) and—if one has children—chauffeur (try getting a cab at 5:00), baby-sitter (they eat you out of house and home), and teacher (private tutoring, no less). Pay for each of these services individually, and one would have quite a bill! A good job description will show the variety of professional services performed by a DRE. Imagine what these services would cost individually and in the open market!

If the job description lists the DRE as an administrator, then the DRE should receive pay equivalent to that of an administrator. Perhaps there are diocesan scales available in one's diocese to which this can be compared, or a public school scale could be used. If there are two scales, one for elementary and another for secondary, use the one which best identifies the work in the job description. Two things should be noted in using such scales. One is that these scales are usually based on educational background and experience. **One has to meet the requirements of the scale in order to use it**. The other item to be noted is that the salary on the scale should be adapted to coincide with the estimated time one would actually spend in administration. If one estimated that as a DRE about one-fourth of one's time would be in administration, then one-fourth of the scale may be used in computing a comparable salary for the DRE.

If the job description includes teaching tasks, it could probably be assumed that most of the teaching will center on adults. In fact, if teacher training is involved, most of these people will probably be high school graduates at the least. This would put most of the teaching done by a DRE at the college level, even if it is only at the first year of college level. Check out the local scale for college personnel in the geographic area. Rate yourself on the basis of professional preparation and years of experience: instructor, assistant professor, or full professor. Again, the scale can only be used if one meets the necessary criteria, and the scale must be adapted to the number of teaching hours involved.

The DRE is also a planner, designer, and consultant. Ever hire a consultant? Ever get free medical consultation or legal advice? These services cost enormously. Yet individual people, businesses, organizations, and even the Church are willing to pay the high price to obtain them. However, it would be unfair to make a direct comparison of these payments with those provided to the DRE. Consultation fees are higher than the actual per hour wage because consultants have overhead expenses and payrolls which the DRE would not have. Nevertheless, some reasonable comparison could be made with these professions in the given geographic situation and could form the basis for comparable remuneration of services.

All three of the areas used in this job description model require the services of professionals. If a parish had to hire three individual people to complete these tasks, the cost would be staggering. If parishes expect DREs to be qualified for the job, that is, have at least a college education, then parishes should also be willing to pay for these professional services.

I am not suggesting that a DRE should be paid the combined salary of an administrator, instructor, and consultant. Nor am I suggesting that a DRE should be compensated the full value of what these services would be worth on an hourly basis in the marketplace. What I am suggesting is that these professions could be used as a basis for arriving at a reasonable scale of compensation for DREs. The comparison with such services justifies DREs receiving higher salaries than most are getting now. However, as the full value of these services is tempered with a sense of dedication and service to the Word, the actual salaries will probably fall below their full market value, and rightly so.

BENEFITS

Salaries represent the single largest amount of compensation for services, but they are not the only ones to be considered. Other benefits which might be negotiated are as follows:

Health Insurance—Normally the employer should pay for complete health insurance coverage of the employee and, in many cases, of the employee's family as well.

Life Insurance—a policy should provide for at least the equal value of one year's salary.

Pension—Usually these are large group plans which a diocese may have for its personnel. The plans often have minimum age requirements for participation and a minimum number of years for full benefits to be accrued.

Car or Mileage Allowance—This is a negotiable item which should be considered if travel is absolutely necessary for the proclamation of the Word in that parish.

Vacations—Regular school holidays, such as Christmas and Easter, plus two or three weeks during the summer is not unreasonable.

Sick Days—One sick day per month accumulative to 120 is within reason. Provision for doctor's verification for more than three consecutive sick days is justifiable.

Days Off—It is easy for DREs to get caught up in a runaway schedule which does not allow for any complete days off. Provisions should be made for at least two complete days off per week, even if these days are not on a weekend. This item could be included here as well as in the job description.

Personal Days—This is a negotiable item which usually does not include more than three days per year, non-accumulative.

PROFESSIONAL BENEFITS

Office—"Adequate" office space is needed for one to carry out the tasks of a DRE. However, "adequate" is subject to interpretation and is negotiable: one telephone or two? electric or manual typewriter? duplicating machine? space? Whatever is reasonable for the proclamation of the Word should be provided.

Secretarial Staff—Depending upon the size and nature of the programs, one can negotiate for part- or full-time secretarial assistance.

Continuing Education—Amounts can vary depending upon

costs in a particular locality, but it is not unreasonable to receive compensation for three credits per year.

Workshops—If one is expected as part of the job description to participate in workshops related to religious education, then it is legitimate to have the parish pay the cost of these workshops.

Membership Fees—Payment of membership fees in local or national groups is negotiable.

Continuing Education Time—If one is going to attend workshops or seminars, should this be part of one's vacation time or should it be provided for otherwise? At least one week would not seem unreasonable.

Staff Meetings—A written description of opportunities to participate in staff meetings or at least having an allotted time each week or month to meet with the pastor can serve as a reminder to both parties of the need for ongoing communication. The amount of time required would depend upon needs and circumstances.

Priestly Support—Putting into writing something like, "The parish priests shall conduct one weekly religious education class at each grade level at times mutually agreeable," at least serves as a start for obtaining supportive help in an area which is sometimes neglected. Again, the need for this depends upon individual circumstances.

The personal and professional benefits are above and beyond the salary compensation. However, some of the items may be included in a salary, such as educational expenses or insurance fees. If these are included in the salary, then both parties should be aware of that.

All manner of payments should be clearly stated in writing. Salaries should be stated as being paid in equal amounts at specified times, such as, twenty-four equal payments paid on the fifteenth and the last day of the month. I once saw a contract which simply stated that, "The DRE shall be paid the annual sum of X amount of dollars." No provision was made for the manner of payment. Should it then be paid only when the Sunday collection was good?

Remember also that employers have certain legal obligations, such as paying part of the social security tax and other taxes which apply.

ALL DRES?

One question which is certainly justified in a discussion of salaries and benefits for DREs is, "Should suggested guidelines apply equally to both lay and religious who are hired as DREs?" Members of religious communities have traditionally worked for low salaries. However, this situation is changing, and even though salaries paid to religious are lower than those paid to lay persons, they are on the rise. Religious may rightly say that they do not need as high a salary as lay persons. Even a single lay person may claim a need for a lower salary than a married one who is supporting a family. What then is the solution?

A suggestion is that whatever scale is drawn up should be paid equally to **any** DRE without discriminating against status, that is, lay married, lay single, male, female, or religious. If the salary is justified for the service provided, then one is entitled to it. What a person wishes to do with that compensation is his or her own business.

A religious, by commitment to a larger community, may return all or part of the salary back to the community. The community then has an obligation to use that money in a manner consistent with the gospel. Perhaps a portion of it could be returned to the parish from which it was originally received. So it could be also with a lay person. If one feels that the compensation received is more than one needs to proclaim the gospel without obstruction, then one could return the money. Perhaps the returned portion could be specially earmarked for a specific purpose in the parish which the DRE feels is a worthy cause, or it could be combined with excess funds from other DREs to support a parish which otherwise would not be able to afford a director.

The method behind this madness in allowing an equitable salary to be paid to all who are in the profession is that those who need the greater sum have it available without seeming to be an added burden on the parish. Those who need less have the opportunity to use the extra amount for furthering the work of the Kingdom in whatever way they choose.

Another materialistic note may be added here. Contributed services are not tax deductible. Monetary donations are. Also, for whatever purposes they serve, contributed services are rarely recorded in parish books. Collections are. This is not the ideal state of the Kingdom, just the reality of a materialistic society of which the Church is a part.

CONCLUSION

A well prepared job description should form the basis for negotiating the amount of compensation. This compensation is also contingent upon professional preparation and experience.

Diocesan guidelines for salary scales should take into account the exact nature of the work and a just compensation for that work. These guidelines should not be drawn up in isolation, but they should involve DREs and other parish representatives. If diocesan support is not available, then DREs will have to rely on their concern and responsibility for each other, perhaps through professional organizations, to arrive at these guidelines.

This article first appeared in PACE in 1978. The author, DARYL OLSZEWSKI, is Director of Religious Education at Mary, Queen of Heaven Parish in West Allis, Wisconsin. This article is one of a series which appeared in its entirety in PACE 9.

11
Your First Year as a DRE— Handling Its Frustrations

Matthias Neuman

As we are all well aware, a goodly number of people who move into a career in out-of-school religious education experience sharp frustrations in their first year of work. The uncertainties of a new job and new tasks cause understandable anxieties, but many new DREs also feel a vague but deep sense of frustration which causes severe disillusionment about their fitness for this work, or its fitness for them. The more unidentifiable the source of this frustration, the higher the anxiety level produced by it and the more hope diminishes. This phenomenon, I might add, seems to be particularly evident in school teachers who transfer into full-time work as parish or diocesan directors or supervisors of religious education programs.

Encountering such frustration can be a critical moment in the career of a religious educator. His or her personal spirituality is deeply affected, for hope functions as a necessary substrate of all Christian virtue. Without a lively hope, an inner apathy quickly sets in. Moreover, because of the leadership position of the religious educator, it is essential to resolve such a crisis of hope. Mounting frustration and anxiety obviously do not help the planting and nourishing of good trusting relationships between the new DRE and other diocesan and parish personnel. The effect too often is the rapid demise of a scarcely-begun career in religious education. This state of affairs demands serious consideration.

Fortunately for our purposes, the functioning of hope in human life (its appearance and growth as well as its diminishing and loss) has been the object of much recent study by psychologists. In engaging in any occupation or lifestyle, they suggest, we are motivated, first, by a **dominant hope,** expressing our main goals. Usually this hope is rather clearly articulated and pursued, even though it may be expressed in images or symbols rather than being worked out into a logically reasoned position. But, in addition to this dominant hope, such occupations as those of doctors, lawyers, and educators offer people a number of **secondary hopes** which function to support and nourish the dominant hope but are also legitimate expectations in themselves. These secondary hopes are usually connected with the more concrete aspects of an occupation. They are rooted in experiential knowledge of one's own abilities, and are fed by satisfactions gained from the repeated use of these abilities.

Secondary hopes, then, look at continual but less basic realizations. For this very reason, they often go unnoticed and are taken for granted when a person considers what he or she "really wants to accomplish." For example, a young woman who is a wife and mother may possess a dominant hope to fulfill these tasks to the best of her ability; she symbolizes this hope in the major acts of love occurring between her and her husband and children. But she also has many secondary hopes, and the satisfactions that their fulfillment gives her, which encourage and support that major hope: e.g., the hope of exercising her abilities as a cook and housekeeper, and as a member of her community. Often these unacknowledged hopes form a necessary foundation for the continued pursuit of the dominant hope.

Obviously, then, when a person changes occupation or adds a significant new job to what he or she is already doing, the hitherto dominant hope must be adjusted, a new expectation moves to the center of awareness. But the transition process also usually weakens or eliminates the day-by-day fulfillment of the concrete, secondary hopes which have exerted a strong but probably unrealized influence on the person's consciousness. As a result, the dominant hope too frequently begins to be significantly diminished, and the person does not know why he or she suddenly experiences confusion and uncertainty about a goal which was so ardently sought only a few months before. Radical frustration and depression may soon follow, if this diminishment is unchecked. To continue the example mentioned above, let us say that the young mother takes a part-time job. While desiring to continue to pursue her dominant hope of being a good wife and mother, her new occupation leaves her no time for creative cooking, housekeeping becomes a burden, and she has to drop her involvement in community affairs. In such circumstances, her dominant hope will be threatened.

I suggest, therefore, that a good deal of the frustration so often experienced by individuals entering full-time jobs in religious education for the first time stems from the non-fulfillment of the secondary hopes connected with their previous occupations. This would be particularly the case when they move from a job in which they had a good deal of success. Persons moving from a regular teaching job in a school into the field of out-of-school religious education often fit this description. When they enter this new field, they have a good feeling about their success as teachers, and do not realize the extent to which this success nourished their primary hope of giving a religious witness—the hope which they expected to pursue even more ardently in a full-time, explicitly "religious" educational ministry. But in their first year's work, they do not experience the same fulfillment of those secondary hopes which they had come to assume from their work in the classroom. These might include hopes for: direct and positive praise from students; an established and comfortable schedule interweaving their work and their personal lives; recognition of their abilities by other teachers; a sense of control and command over the material to be taught in the classroom.

It is precisely such secondary hopes which are not fulfilled in their new situation as DREs. They have to spend a great deal of time in administration, rather than teaching. The people with whom they work are waiting to see how they will perform and give them little positive feedback. The success of new programs is very uncertain. New personal and professional relationships must be formed and a new rhythm of life established, probably far less regular than their former one. Lacking the accustomed fulfillment of their secondary hopes, then, they begin to feel an undefined frustration which challenges their dominant hope. They begin to wonder, "What really is the value of my Christian witness in this situation which I thought would provide a wider scope for it?"

Psychological studies treating the interaction of hope and frustration in job transitions can provide some useful suggestions on how to handle this crisis. First of all, an adequate resolution of the problem demands more than an intellectual grasp of it. It requires taking action to desensitize oneself to one's previous expectations, rooted as they have become in physical habits. Secondly, one must cultivate a willingness to balance the present nonfulfillment of expectations with the gradual development of new secondary hopes. This takes time and patience.

To new DREs, especially those coming from a school situation, I would therefore suggest: learn to anticipate frustration, especially that vague frustration the source of which cannot be completely identified and, when you do experience it, consciously accept the necessity of living with it for a while. This task can become a realistic part of your daily prayer life.

Become aware also that a shift in your secondary hopes will probably be necessary sooner or later. This necessity might initiate a serious process of self-examination, searching out the hidden, partially known, gratifications of a past job and lifestyle. With the help of a perceptive director or friend, this self-examination can result in a true purification of life. Learn to speak openly about "known and recognized needs" to someone who can give support in these areas. In daily prayer, allow time for a reflective review of life. Include both past months and previous occupation. What really gave you satisfaction in the past? Make this theme a topic of shared prayer. Introduce the difficulties of "changing a life hope" into the context of daily petitions. Take the time to discover new talents, new satisfactions, and the courage to develop new hopes.

As you work, if frustration continues to mount, don't hesitate to make adjustments in the overall planning of programs. Put your main efforts in those areas in which existing programs are most successful. Learn to develop strengths and survive with weaknesses. Often the weak areas will improve when the personal confidence and hope of the DRE are increased by success in already strong areas. It isn't necessary to spread oneself thin in trying to do the same high quality of work in all the areas of your responsibility. When frustration becomes sharp, concentrate on what you know is going well. Encourage others concerned to take pride in that successful area. New secondary hopes will slowly be constructed by this tactic.

In the end, the venture of moving into a career in religious education, rightly viewed and correctly handled, can be a tool for valid self-discovery and authentic spiritual growth. What happens in this limited sphere can have a wider application in your life, particularly to future changes in occupation and lifestyle.

The final purpose of these reflections is a simple one: to help people carry out a more effective ministry. If these thoughts provide some new religious educators with a little more patience, perseverance, and courage to live through their first-year frustrations, this intent will have been served.

This article first appeared in PACE in 1976. The author, REV. MATTHIAS NEUMAN, OSB, is a professor of systematic theology at St. Meinrad's Seminary and director of the master of religious education program.

12
The Advocate: A Role of the Local Association

Don Kurre

Up until now parish administrators of religious education/DREs/ PCREs have been all but silent regarding their fundamental plight and the plight of their profession. Administrators of religious education, as a group, have done little effectively to improve the environments in which they work. Because of low pay, inadequate working materials, faulty relationships with boards of education and pastors, it is not unusual to see DREs changing parishes every two or three years. Nor is it unusual to see qualified, competent professionals changing fields after a short exploratory stand as an administrator of religious education. Consequently, the Association of Parish Administrators of Religious Education (APARE) in the Archdiocese of Indianapolis is finding it necessary to face the difficult question: what can we as an association do to help keep DREs in parishes? Posing this question has caused the association to ask a further and more probing question: what will be the future role of the association? Arriving at this question has been for the association a very long and often painful quest.

APARE began four years ago in response to the individual administrators' needs for support and practical training for ministry in a young field. The DREs had immediate and pressing needs for support and training for their on-the-job activities. Many administrators found themselves in a profession and a parish environment lacking definition and scope. The need to find, to sharpen, and to adapt skills appropriate to the ministry of religious education was their concern. The association was born out of these needs.

As the individual administrator grows up—moves toward the state of "precision" foreseen by Maria Harris—the role of the association changes.[1] The local association will continue to provide administrators with in-service opportunities and support. These activities, which at one time were the main reason for the association's existence, have begun to form the foundation upon which the activities of the association of the future will be built.

If the future role of the local association is to be understood, it is important to realize that APARE, like other associations, has moved from an informal gathering of co-workers to a formal constitution-directed association. The association has been given the responsibility of offering services to the DREs, for the DREs, and— with the diocesan director of religious education—providing for their growth and the growth of the profession within the diocese. That is to say, the association has been given, by its members, an identity, a role, and a life of its own. The association is just beginning to understand this life and its role within the profession.

There are many possible roles for the association of the future. We will focus here on the one born from the most pressing current need of the administrator, i.e., the advocate role.

As I have said, at birth the association was concerned mainly with its members, providing support and training. It seems to me that the movement toward precision is carrying the association movement in a more outwardly focused direction. While the larger Church community felt the indirect results of the association's work in the past, the target of the association was the religious educator himself or herself. For the profession (now with its own house in a semblance of order or at least with a sense of direction) to continue to grow and be effective within the Church, the association will be, and is, targeting more of its activity to groups and persons outside itself.

For example, it has become necessary for the association to collaborate with the diocese in the formation of norms for hiring, maintaining, and terminating contractual agreements with parishes. The association is beginning to understand that it has a role to play in disputes that develop between individual DREs and parishes. The

---

[1]Maria Harris, "The Future of the Profession from a Catholic Perspective," in **Parish Religious Education**, ed. by Maria Harris (New York: Paulist Press, 1978), pp. 220-221.

association is taking the initiative and responsibility for defining and determining working conditions for the DRE at the local level. From my point of view, the future of the profession will depend not only upon the ability of the DRE to do his/her job effectively, but also upon the ability of the association to be an advocate for the profession and the professional.

The future of the profession depends in large part on the way the Church community as a whole sees, deals with, and uses the professional religious education administrator. The association must, therefore, begin to move into the larger arena, as an advocate. The association, because it is able to devote the time and resources necessary to listen to and interpret the needs and concerns of the working religious educator, will take the initiative in establishing the communicating norms for the professional religious education field in a given area. Up until now those outside the profession—for example, the diocesan office of education—have set norms. Now the association will be able to effectively reach the diocesan office, parish boards of education, pastors, principals, parish staff, as well as the total Catholic community. The association will represent and explain the tasks, needs, concerns, and excitements of the professional religious educator to the larger Church community.

Furthermore, by accepting its advocacy role, the local association will begin to collaborate with regional and national associations so that the overall goals of the association may be realized within the total Church community. If these goals are to be realized, the association will have to lead the way in collaborating with diocesan offices, principals' associations, schools, and other organizations in developing programs, educational opportunities, and worship experiences which share and develop visions, norms, and understanding. In such ways, the association can show DREs effective new ways of relating to boards of education, to parish councils, to pastors, to principals, and to the Catholic community as a whole.

How will the local parish administrator of religious education benefit from the association's new movement? First, through their association, the local DREs will be taking the initiative in determining the norms and scope of the field. As a result, they will develop a greater sense of corporate and individual pride and self-confidence. This deepened sense of self-confidence will increase the effectiveness with which they accomplish their work. As we all know, improved self-understanding and effectiveness will improve the fundamental satisfaction and enjoyment that DREs find in their ministry. It has been shown clearly that increased job satisfaction leads to greater longevity within a particular job or profession.

Second, the local DREs will benefit because those members of a parish responsible for hiring and maintaining DREs and the DREs themselves will share expectations of each other that are compatible. As a result, the unhealthy tension, conflict, and uncertainties—typical of the relationship between many religious educators and the parishes—will be reduced or eliminated.

Third, as the norms for DREs are established and implemented, religious education administrators will enjoy the greater sense of job security that results from clear expectations, role definitions, and adequate compensations. When combined, the prospect of career pride and job security will function to draw "professional" religious educators to the field and the diocese. As qualified and competent people enter the field, those administrators already active in the profession will benefit from the experience, vision, and skill that this new blood will bring to the area.

Finally, as norms and expectations are clarified, adequate compensation given, and working conditions improve, the field will become stable enough to make positive contributions to the Church's mission to teach as Jesus did. Furthermore, parishes will find it more attractive to call upon members of a stabilized profession to assist them in meeting their total Catholic educational goals.

There are and will be many tasks, roles, and questions for the association of the future to address. Nevertheless, the members of the religious education administrators' profession must respect themselves enough to see that adequate norms and expectations are set and followed. The association as advocate is ideally suited to be the vehicle through which these administrators can and must establish and promulgate these norms. Only then will the association be able to develop its full role for the future.

This article first appeared in PACE in 1980. The author, DON KURRE, is currently employed as a director of religious education at St. Lawrence Parish in Indianapolis and is president of the Archdiocesan Association of Parish Administrators of Religious Education (APARE).